Worship & Song

Singer's Edition

Abingdon Press
Nashville

INTRODUCTION

Worship in the Christian church in the United States, once quite homogenous, is becoming increasingly diverse. Some local churches offer different styles of worship in different services. Others focus exclusively on one style. Still others incorporate elements of several styles in the same service. And congregational worship music reflects that diversity of worship style and practice.

Worship & Song has been compiled to supplement hymnals and songbooks currently in use, particularly *The United Methodist Hymnal* (1989) and *The Faith We Sing* (2000). There are no duplications of content between *Worship & Song* and either of its predecessors. The music is intended to be representative of the breadth of current worship practice, providing new material in several musical genres and including older material not appearing in former United Methodist collections. It also provides music from many different styles to churches that offer primarily one worship style who desire to broaden their repertoire. Praise music, recently written hymns, gospel songs, world music, music from various ethnic traditions, music from the Taizé and Iona communities, and various pieces of service music are all included.

The Pew Edition is intended for congregational use; songs intended to be sung in unison (or in parts) are printed in unison (or in parts). The Accompaniment Edition is for keyboard players, with some songs given both stylistic and simplified versions; it also includes basic chord symbols for guitarists. The Singer's Edition is intended for choirs and includes some choral harmonizations, descants, and endings. The Leader's Edition is a photographic enlargement of the Pew Edition allowing leaders to see it from a podium; it also includes descriptions of each song and several additional indexes. The Worship Resources Edition contains no music but rather over 200 prayers, litanies, affirmations, and other acts of worship. The Presentation Edition includes the words of all songs and worship resources on electronic files suitable for projection. An Internet Edition will include online versions of the majority of the books' contents for downloading. It will also allow for the continual addition of new songs and prayers even after original publication.

Worship hymns and songs and prayers are constantly being written and used. The publication of *Worship & Song* creates a snapshot of the rich variety of resources available to the church. It is my prayer that the print, digital, and Internet editions of *Worship & Song*, along with those future materials still to be published, will enrich your faith journey.

Gary Alan Smith
General Editor and Project Director

O For a Thousand Tongues to Sing 3001

WORDS: Charles Wesley
MUSIC: Mark A. Miller

AZMON'S GHOST
CM

Music © 2000 Abingdon Press, admin. by The Copyright Company

3002 Blessed Be Your Name

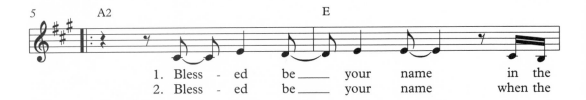

1. Bless - ed be ____ your name in the
2. Bless - ed be ____ your name when the

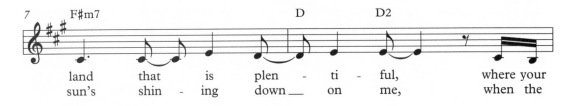

land that is plen - ti - ful, where your
sun's shin - ing down ____ on me, when the

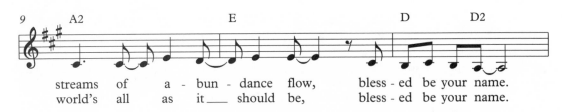

streams of a - bun - dance flow, bless - ed be your name.
world's all as it ____ should be, bless - ed be your name.

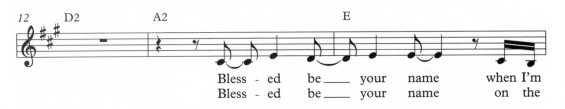

Bless - ed be ____ your name when I'm
Bless - ed be ____ your name on the

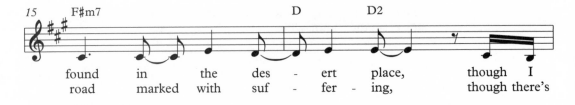

found in the des - ert place, though I
road marked with suf - fer - ing, though there's

walk through the wil - der - ness, bless - ed be your name.
pain in the of - fer - ing, bless - ed be your name.

WORDS: Matt Redman and Beth Redman
MUSIC: Matt Redman and Beth Redman

BLESSED BE YOUR NAME
Irr. with Refrain

3003

How Great Is Our God

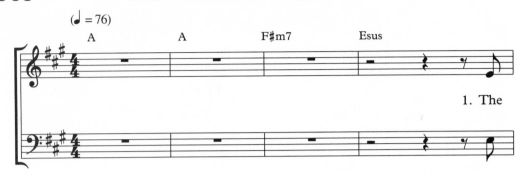

WORDS: Chris Tomlin, Jesse Reeves, and Ed Cash
MUSIC: Chris Tomlin, Jesse Reeves, and Ed Cash

HOW GREAT IS OUR GOD
Irr. with Refrain

heart will sing, "How great _ is our God!" _

3004 Step by Step

(♩ = 92-100)

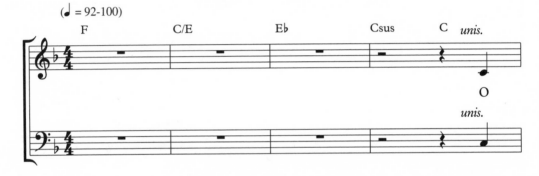

O

unis.

unis.

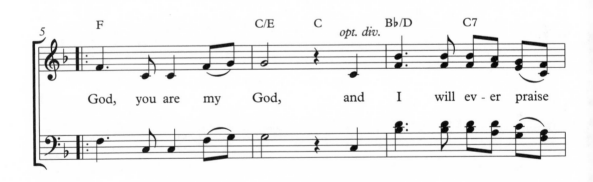

God, you are my God, and I will ev-er praise

you. O God, you are my God, and

(unis.)

WORDS: David Strasser
MUSIC: David Strasser

STEP BY STEP
Irr.

© 1991 Universal Songs-MGB Songs (ASCAP) and Kid Brother of St. Frank Publishing

3005 Fill Us with Your Love, O Lord

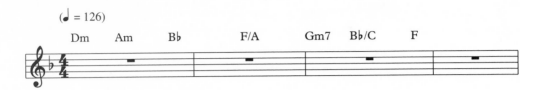

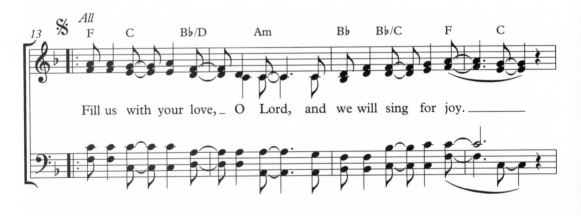

WORDS: Carol Browning (Ps. 90:12-17)
MUSIC: Carol Browning

FILL US
Irr. with Refrain

The English translation of the psalm response from *Lectionary for Music* © 1969, 1981, 1977 ICEL
Music © 2001 GIA Publications, Inc.

CODA

49 *All a cappella (optional)*

Fill us with your love, __ O Lord, and we will sing for joy. _____

53

Fill us with your love, __ O Lord, and we will sing for joy. __

3006 Alleluia

D   A/C♯   G2/B   D/A   G   D/F♯   A   D

Al - le - lu - ia!   Al - le - lu - ia!

9   D   A/C♯   G2/B   D/A   G   D/F♯   A   D

Al - le - lu - ia!   Al - le - lu - ia!

WORDS: Traditional liturgical text
MUSIC: Norah Duncan IV

ALLELUIA (DUNCAN)
44.44

Music © 1987 GIA Publications, Inc.

Laudate Dominum
(Sing, Praise and Bless the Lord)

3007

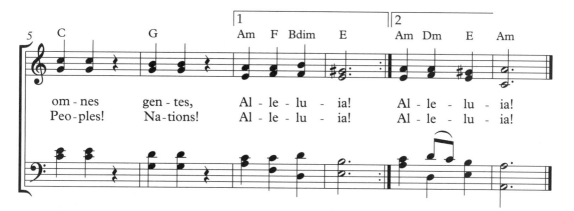

Latin Lau - da - te Do - mi - num, lau - da - te Do - mi - num,
English Sing, praise and bless the Lord. Sing, praise and bless the Lord.

om - nes gen - tes, Al - le - lu - ia! Al - le - lu - ia!
Peo - ples! Na - tions! Al - le - lu - ia! Al - le - lu - ia!

WORDS: The Community of Taizé
MUSIC: Jacques Berthier

LAUDATE DOMINUM
66.44

Open the Eyes of My Heart

3008

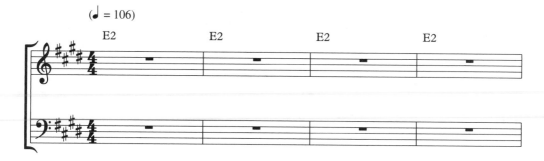

WORDS: Paul Baloche
MUSIC: Paul Baloche

EYES OF MY HEART
Irr.

3009 Praise God for This Holy Ground

1. Praise God for this ho - ly ground,
2. Praise God in whose word we find
3. Praise God who through Christ makes known
4. Praise God's Spir - it who be - friends,
5. Though praise ends, praise is be - gun

Refrain

place and peo - ple, sight and sound.
food for bod - y, soul, and mind.
all are loved and called God's own. Hal - le - lu - jah! Hal - le - lu - jah!
rais - es, hum - bles, breaks, and mends.
where God's will is glad - ly done.

Hal-le-lu-jah! God's good-ness is e - ter - nal.

WORDS: John L. Bell
MUSIC: John L. Bell

© 2002 WGRG, Iona Community (Scotland), admin. by GIA Publications, Inc.

HEYMONYSTRAAT
77 with Refrain

3010 Sing of the Lord's Goodness

Joyfully MIDI: PEDAL: TYMPANI OR STR. BASS

1. Sing of the Lord's good-ness, Fa - ther of all wis-dom,
2. Pow - er he has wield - ed, hon - or is his gar - ment,
3. Cour - age in our dark-ness, com - fort in our sor - row,
4. Praise him with your sing - ing, praise him with the trum-pet,

WORDS: Ernest Sands
MUSIC: Ernest Sands; descant arr. by Christopher Walker; trumpet arr. by Paul Inwood

© 1981 Ernest Sands, admin. by OCP Publications

THE LORD'S GOODNESS
12 7.12 7 with Refrain

3011

All My Days

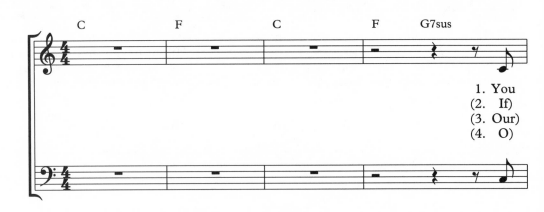

know my words be-fore they're said. You know my need and
I should fly be-yond the dawn, the dark-ness will not
ev-ery thought, each word we say, the whole of time, the
mend my heart and free my voice. From sin re-leased; I

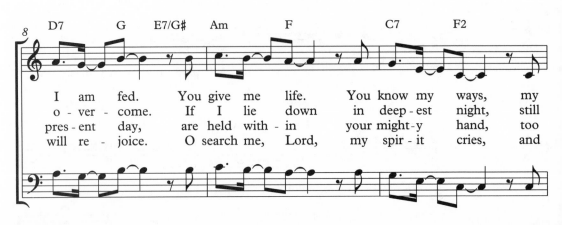

I am fed. You give me life. You know my ways, my
o-ver-come. If I lie down in deep-est night, still
pres-ent day, are held with-in your might-y hand, too
will re-joice. O search me, Lord, my spir-it cries, and

WORDS: Laurie Zelman
MUSIC: Mark A. Miller

HIXON
88.88

11 C/G   F/A   *div.* Eaug   Am   C7/G   C/F   Dm7   *unis.*

strength, my   path,   for   all   my   days,   my strength, my   path,   for
you   are   there,   my Lord,   my   light,   still   you   are   there,   my
won - der - ful   to com - pre - hend,   too won - der - ful   to
let   my   song   of praise a - rise,   and   let   my   song   of

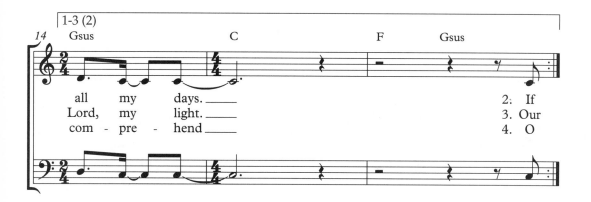

1-3 (2)

14 Gsus   C   F   Gsus

all   my   days. _____   2: If
Lord,   my   light. _____   3. Our
com - pre - hend _____   4. O

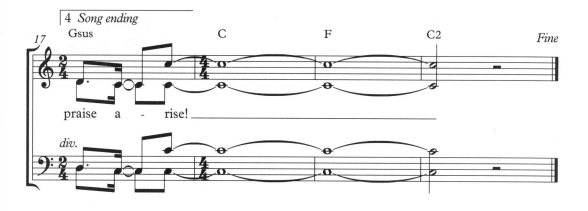

4 *Song ending*

17 Gsus   C   F   C2   *Fine*

praise a - rise! _____

div.

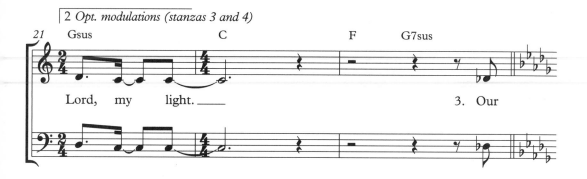

2 *Opt. modulations (stanzas 3 and 4)*

21 Gsus   C   F   G7sus

Lord,   my   light. _____   3. Our

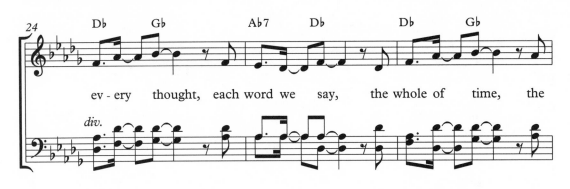

ev - ery thought, each word we say, the whole of time, the

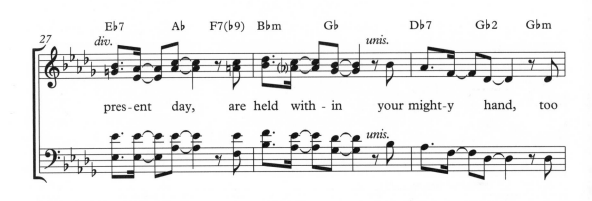

pres - ent day, are held with - in your might-y hand, too

won - der - ful to com - pre - hend, too won - der - ful to

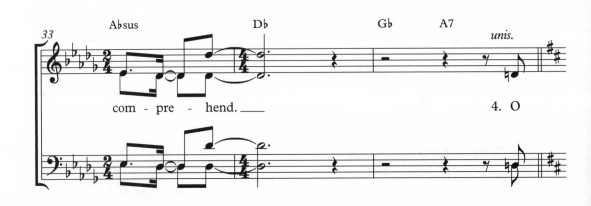

com - pre - hend. _____ 4. O

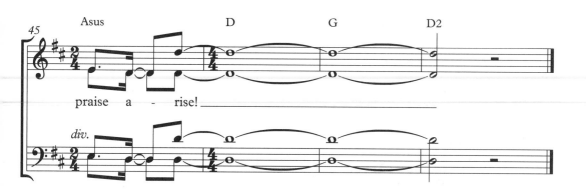

3012   When Words Alone Cannot Express

1. When words a-lone can-not ex-press all
2. When speech e-rodes and tem-pers flare, when
3. When bread is bro-ken, wine is poured, when
4. With-in each sea-son of our lives, when

that our hearts ache to con-fess, bring mu-sic! Al-le-
peace gives way to i-dle dare, bring mu-sic! Al-le-
we en-coun-ter Christ the Lord, bring mu-sic! Al-le-
ev-ery pas-sage-way ar-rives, bring mu-sic! Al-le-

lu - ia! Bring mel-o-dy and rhyth-mic fire! Bring
lu - ia! Let psalms re-store our mem-o-ry that
lu - ia! When chil-dren teach us how to pray, when
lu - ia! Sing when the in-fant draws a breath; sing

in-stru-ments, bring bells and choir! Bring mu-sic! Al-le-
God has made us to be free! Bring mu-sic! Al-le-
sim-ple he-roes show the way, bring mu-sic! Al-le-
when the el-der yields to death. Bring mu-sic! Al-le-

WORDS: John Thornburg
MUSIC: *Geistliche Kirchengesänge*, 1623; harm. by Ralph Vaughan Williams

LASST UNS ERFREUEN
88.34.88 with Refrain

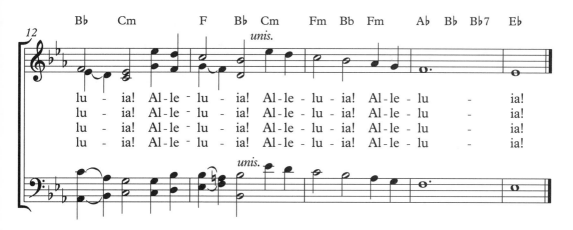

Bb   Cm   F   Bb   Cm   Fm   Bb   Fm   Ab   Bb   Bb7   Eb

unis.

lu - ia! Al - le - lu - ia! Al - le - lu - ia! Al - le - lu - ia!
lu - ia! Al - le - lu - ia! Al - le - lu - ia! Al - le - lu - ia!
lu - ia! Al - le - lu - ia! Al - le - lu - ia! Al - le - lu - ia!
lu - ia! Al - le - lu - ia! Al - le - lu - ia! Al - le - lu - ia!

unis.

Sing the Praise of God Our Maker — 3013

C   Am   Ab   Bb   Eb   F   Cm

1. Sing   the praise of   God   our   Mak - er,   source   of   won - der,
2. Sing   the praise of   Christ   our   Broth - er,   sage   whose words   speak
3. Sing   the praise of   Ho - ly   Spir - it,   spark   in   hu - man

Ab   Bb   C   Am   Ab   Bb   Eb

font   of grace,   gild - er   of   the   vast   ho - ri - zon,
lib - er - ty,   car - pen - ter   of   new   be - gin - nings,
his - to - ry,   res - i - dent   at   font   and   ta - ble,

Fm   Cm   Fm   Gm7   Ab   Bb   C

jewel - er of   un - end - ing   space.
ad - vo - cate   who   sets   us   free.
ar - chi - tect   of   mys - ter - y.

WORDS: John Thornburg
MUSIC: Sally Ann Morris

© 2008 GIA Publications, Inc.

BROTHER
87.87

You Are Good — 3014

(♩ = 126-132)

E   B/E   D/E   A/E

WORDS: Israel Houghton
MUSIC: Israel Houghton

YOU ARE GOOD
Irr.

© 2001 Integrity's Hosanna! Music and Champions for Christ Publishing (Admin. by ICG)

How Great You Are

3015

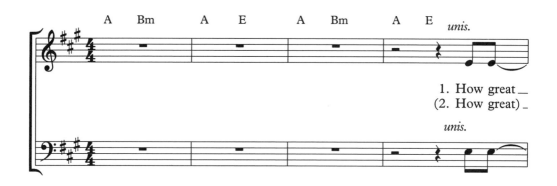

1. How great __
(2. How great) __

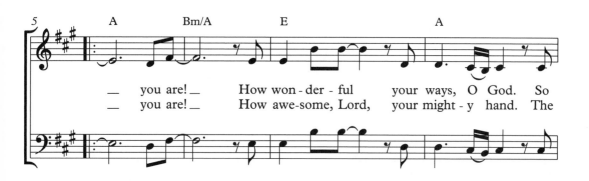

__ you are! __ How won-der-ful your ways, O God. So
__ you are! __ How awe-some, Lord, your might-y hand. The

sings my soul, my Sav - ior, God, to thee. __ How great __
sun, the moon and stars __ you hold in place. __ How great __

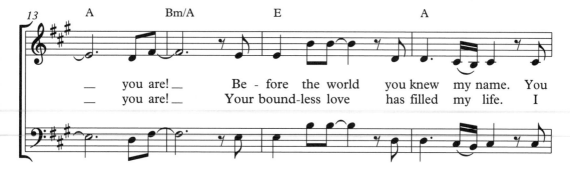

__ you are! __ Be - fore the world you knew my name. You
__ you are! __ Your bound-less love has filled my life. I

WORDS: Phil Posthuma
MUSIC: Phil Posthuma, arr. Jackson Henry

POSTHUMA
4 8 10 D with Refrain

How great you are! ___

3016 What a Mighty God We Serve

What a might - y God we serve.

What a might - y God we serve. An-gels bow be - fore you,

heaven and earth a - dore you. What a might - y God we serve.

WORDS: Traditional African folk song
MUSIC: Traditional African folk song, arr. by Jackson Henry

MIGHTY GOD
Irr.

Arr. © 2010 Jackson Henry

3017 Come, Join the Dance of Trinity

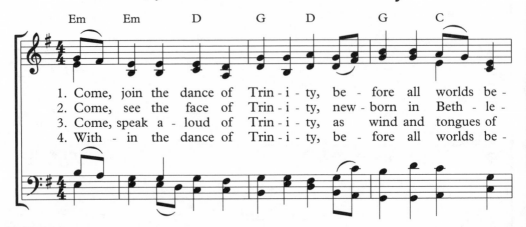

1. Come, join the dance of Trin - i - ty, be - fore all worlds be -
2. Come, see the face of Trin - i - ty, new - born in Beth - le -
3. Come, speak a - loud of Trin - i - ty, as wind and tongues of
4. With - in the dance of Trin - i - ty, be - fore all worlds be -

WORDS: Richard Leach
MUSIC: Trad. English melody; arr. by Ralph Vaughan Williams

KINGSFOLD
CMD

Words © 2001 Selah Publishing Co., Inc.

Creation Sings

1. Cre - a - tion sings! And we are in the
2. Cre - a - tion groans at our dis - cor - dant

mu - sic, the move-ment of God's en - er - gy and
clash - ing: the Spir - it comes with mu - sic as our

art, a lit - ur - gy that links our life to
friend to bring the har - mo - ny of peace and

an - gels, a lit - a - ny that ris - es from the
beau - ty, to teach the tex - tures of the way to

WORDS: Shirley Erena Murray
MUSIC: Traditional Irish melody; transcription by Dean McIntyre

LONDONDERRY AIR
Irr.

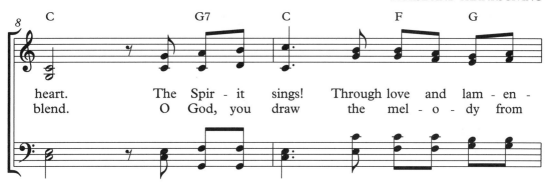

heart. The Spir - it sings! Through love and lam - en -
blend. O God, you draw the mel - o - dy from

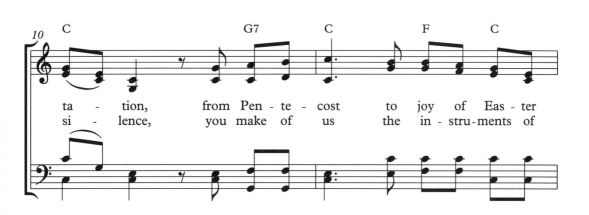

ta - tion, from Pen - te - cost to joy of Eas - ter
si - lence, you make of us the in - stru-ments of

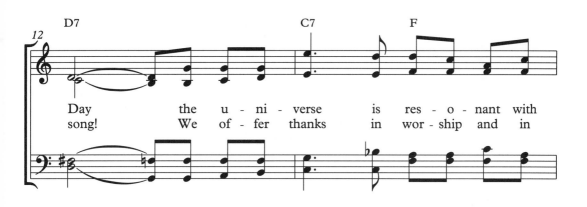

Day the u - ni - verse is res - o - nant with
song! We of - fer thanks in wor - ship and in

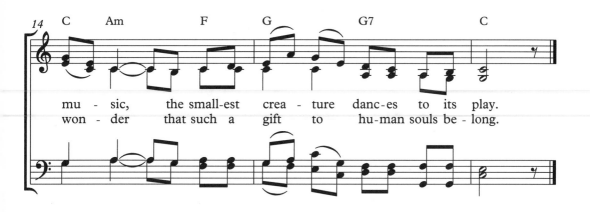

mu - sic, the small-est crea - ture danc-es to its play.
won - der that such a gift to hu - man souls be - long.

3019

Bidden, Unbidden

1. Wheth-er I cry out your name, or I feel all a-lone, a-
2. If I don't feel you a-round, there is no pic-ture and no

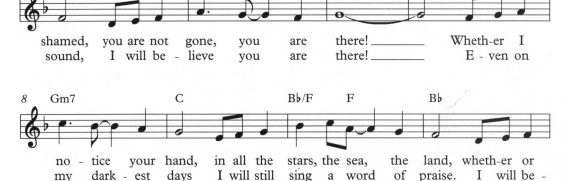

shamed, you are not gone, you are there! _____ Wheth-er I
sound, I will be-lieve you are there! _____ E-ven on

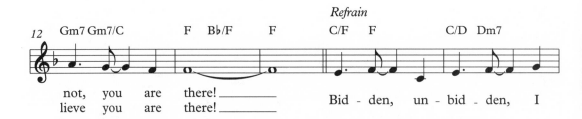

no-tice your hand, in all the stars, the sea, the land, wheth-er or
my dark-est days I will still sing a word of praise. I will be-

Refrain

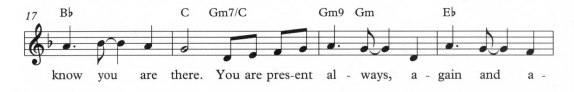

not, you are there! _____ Bid-den, un-bid-den, I
lieve you are there! _____

know you are there. You are pres-ent al-ways, a-gain and a-

gain. _____ If I for-get you, or join you in

prayer, you are pres-ent al-ways for-ev-er. A-men. _____

WORDS: Jenni Lee Boyden and Rusty Edwards
MUSIC: Rusty Edwards

JEWEL
787 D with Refrain

God of the Bible

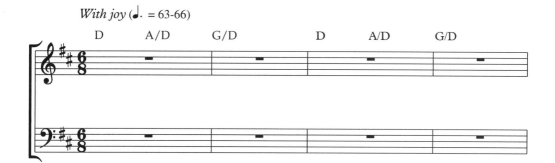

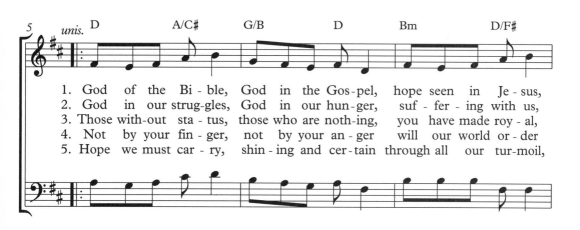

1. God of the Bi - ble, God in the Gos - pel, hope seen in Je - sus,
2. God in our strug - gles, God in our hun - ger, suf - fer - ing with us,
3. Those with-out sta - tus, those who are noth - ing, you have made roy - al,
4. Not by your fin - ger, not by your an - ger will our world or - der
5. Hope we must car - ry, shin - ing and cer - tain through all our tur-moil,

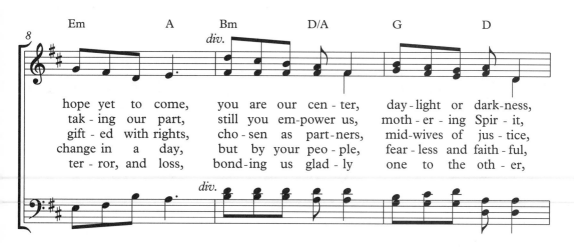

hope yet to come, you are our cen - ter, day-light or dark-ness,
tak - ing our part, still you em-power us, moth - er - ing Spir - it,
gift - ed with rights, cho - sen as part-ners, mid-wives of jus - tice,
change in a day, but by your peo - ple, fear - less and faith - ful,
ter - ror, and loss, bond-ing us glad - ly one to the oth - er,

WORDS: Shirley Erena Murray
MUSIC: Tony E. Alonso

FRESH AS THE MORNING
55.54 D with Refrain

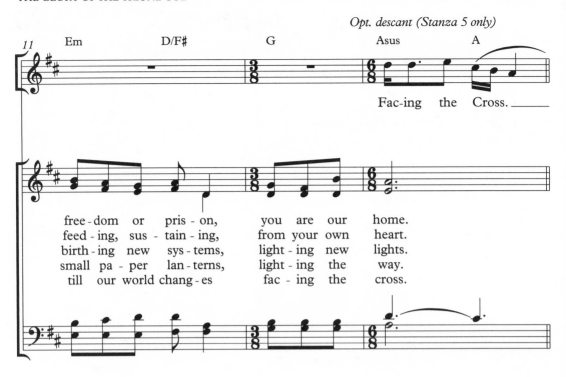

Opt. descant (Stanza 5 only)

Fac-ing the Cross. _____

free - dom or pris - on, you are our home.
feed - ing, sus - tain - ing, from your own heart.
birth - ing new sys - tems, light - ing new lights.
small pa - per lan - terns, light - ing the way.
till our world chang - es fac - ing the cross.

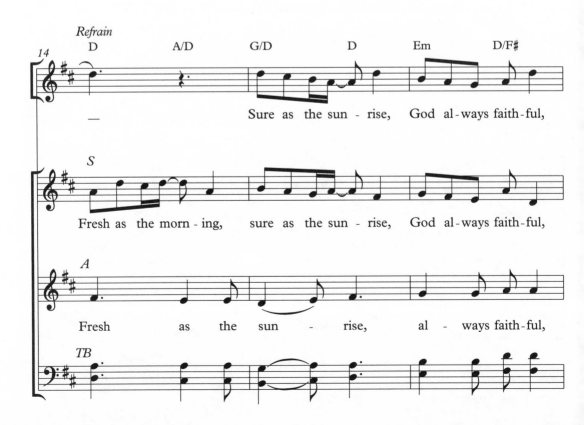

Refrain

Sure as the sun - rise, God al - ways faith-ful,

Fresh as the morn - ing, sure as the sun - rise, God al - ways faith-ful,

Fresh as the sun - rise, al - ways faith-ful,

3021

Everlasting God

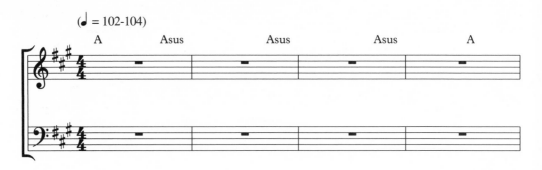

WORDS: Brenton Brown and Ken Riley
MUSIC: Brenton Brown and Ken Riley

EVERLASTING GOD
Irr.

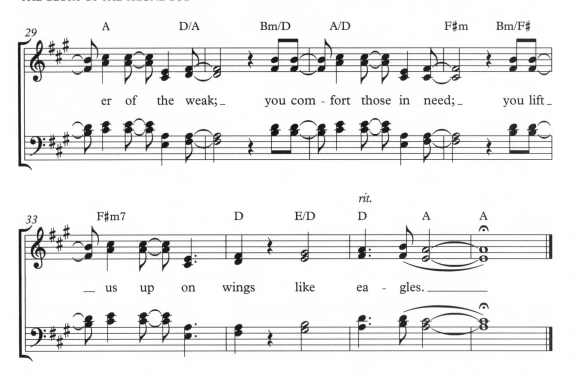

er of the weak; _ you com-fort those in need; _ you lift _

_ us up on wings like ea-gles. _____

3022   Peace of Our Praying

(♩ = 104)

1. Peace of our pray-ing, Song of our sing-ing, Truth of our
2. Peace of our pray-ing, Christ of our cry-ing, Strength of our
3. Peace of our pray-ing, Faith of for-giv-ing, Way of our

tell-ing,   Love of all loves,   Health of our heal-ing,
striv-ing,   Heart of our heart,   Bread of our break-ing,
walk-ing,   King of all kings,   Breath of our breath-ing,

Gift of our giv-ing,   Life of our liv-ing,   Light of all lights.
Wine of our wait-ing,   Blood of our boast-ing,   Death of all death.
Cour-age of car-ing,   Hope of our hop-ing,   Life of all life.

WORDS: Terry W. York
MUSIC: C. David Bolin

PAHOA
55.54 D

Forever

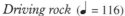

Driving rock (♩ = 116)

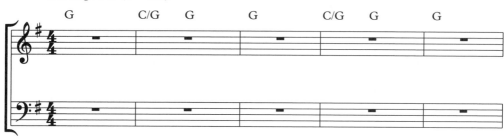

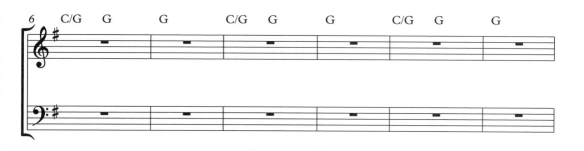

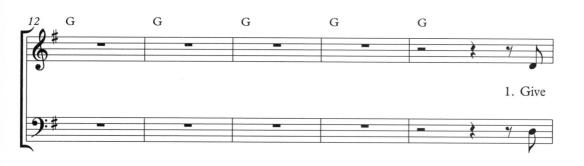

1. Give

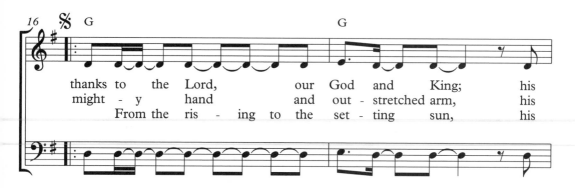

thanks to the Lord, our God and King; his
might - y hand and out - stretched arm, his
From the ris - ing to the set - ting sun, his

WORDS: Chris Tomlin
MUSIC: Chris Tomlin

FOREVER
Irr.

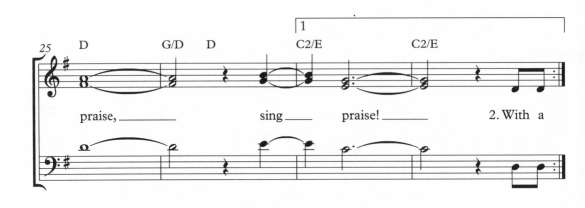

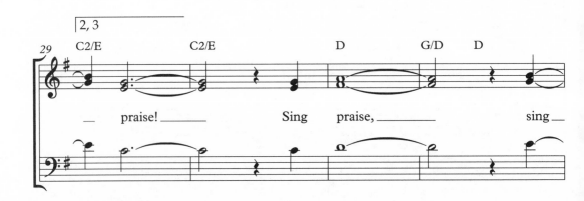

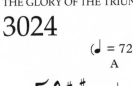

With You, O Lord

WORDS: Community of Taizé (Ps. 36:10)
MUSIC: Jacques Berthier

WITH YOU
11 9.11 9

© 1998 Les Presses de Taizé (France), admin. by GIA Publications, Inc.

Stanzas (*superimposed on ostinato chorale*)

*Choose either part.

MUSIC: Jacques Berthier

© 1998 Les Presses de Taizé (France), admin. by GIA Publications, Inc.

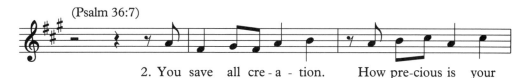

(Psalm 36:7)

2. You save all cre-a-tion. How pre-cious is your

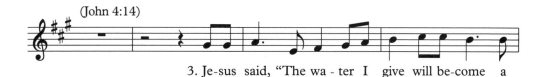

stead-fast love. All peo-ple take ref-uge in you.

(John 4:14)

3. Je-sus said, "The wa-ter I give will be-come a

spring of wa-ter gush-ing up, gush-ing up to life e-ter-nal."

God Is Speaking

3025

(♩ = 76)

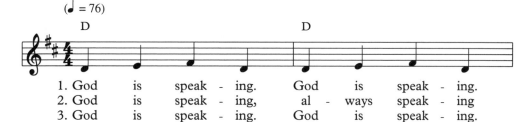

1. God is speak - ing. God is speak - ing.
2. God is speak - ing, al - ways speak - ing
3. God is speak - ing. God is speak - ing.

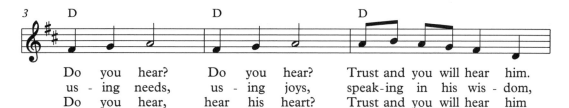

Do you hear? Do you hear? Trust and you will hear him.
us - ing needs, us - ing joys, speak-ing in his wis - dom,
Do you hear, hear his heart? Trust and you will hear him

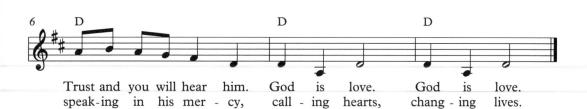

Trust and you will hear him. God is love. God is love.
speak-ing in his mer - cy, call - ing hearts, chang - ing lives.
if you want to hear him. God is love, al - ways love.

WORDS: Ken Bible
MUSIC: Traditional French melody

FRÈRE JACQUES
44.33.66.33

Words © LNWhymns.com (ASCAP), admin. by The Copyright Company

3026 God Is Good, All the Time

WORDS: Dean McIntyre
MUSIC: Dean McIntyre

GOD IS GOOD
99.99

Hallelujah

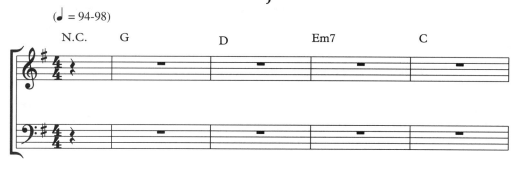

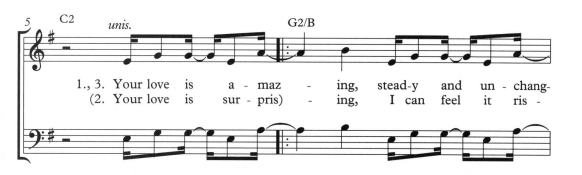

1., 3. Your love is a - maz - ing, stead-y and un - chang-
(2. Your love is sur - pris) - ing, I can feel it ris -

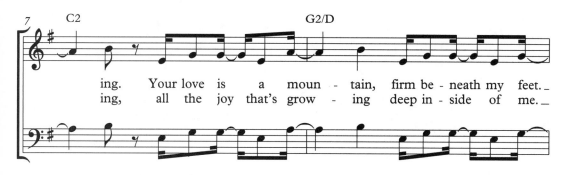

ing. Your love is a moun - tain, firm be - neath my feet. _
ing, all the joy that's grow - ing deep in - side of me. _

— Your love is a mys - tery, how you gent - ly lift___
— Ev - ery time I see___ you all your good-ness shines___

WORDS: Brenton Brown and Brian Doerksen
MUSIC: Brenton Brown and Brian Doerksen

YOUR LOVE IS AMAZING
Irr. with Refrain

3028

Holy Is the Lord

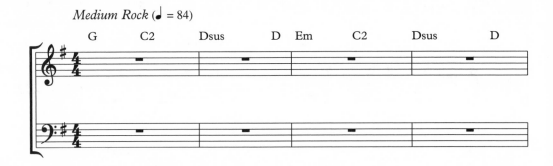

We stand and lift up our hands, __ for the joy __

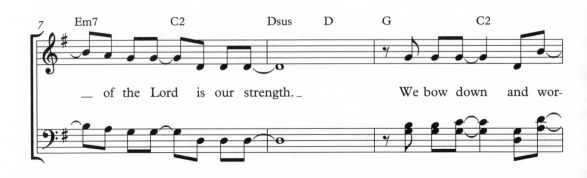

__ of the Lord is our strength. __ We bow down and wor-

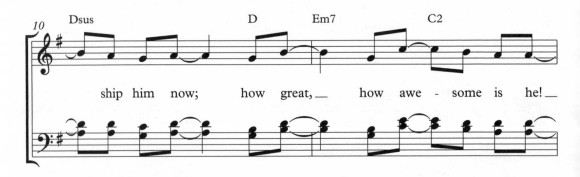

ship him now; how great, __ how awe - some is he! __

WORDS: Chris Tomlin and Louie Giglio
MUSIC: Chris Tomlin and Louie Giglio

GIGLIO
Irr. with Refrain

3029 In the Desert, on God's Mountain

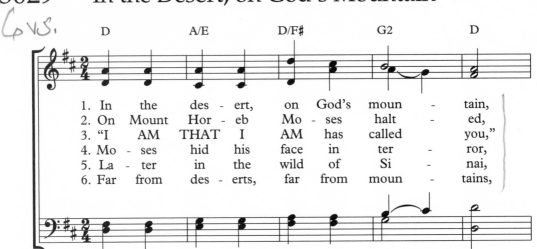

1. In the des - ert, on God's moun - tain,
2. On Mount Hor - eb Mo - ses halt - ed,
3. "I AM THAT I AM has called you,"
4. Mo - ses hid his face in ter - ror,
5. La - ter in the wild of Si - nai,
6. Far from des - erts, far from moun - tains,

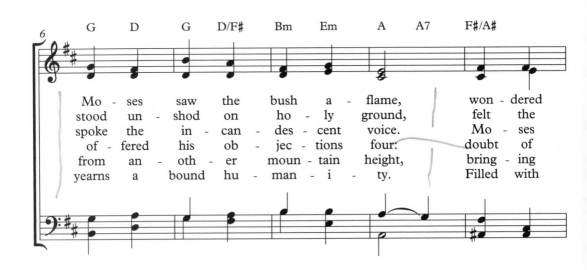

Mo - ses saw the bush a - flame, won - dered
stood un - shod on ho - ly ground, felt the
spoke the in - can - des - cent voice. Mo - ses
of - fered his ob - jec - tions four: doubt of
from an - oth - er moun - tain height, bring - ing
yearns a bound hu - man - i - ty. Filled with

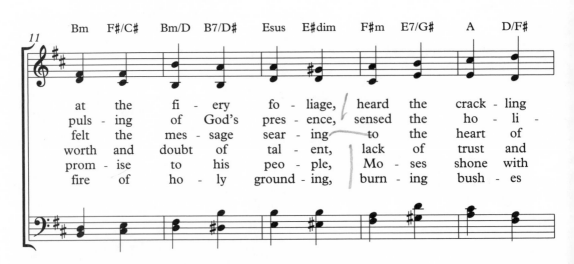

at the fi - ery fo - liage, heard the crack - ling
puls - ing of God's pres - ence, sensed the ho - li -
felt the mes - sage sear - ing to the heart of
worth and doubt of tal - ent, lack of trust and
prom - ise to his peo - ple, Mo - ses shone with
fire of ho - ly ground - ing, burn - ing bush - es

WORDS: Susan Palo Cherwien
MUSIC: John Goss

LAUDA ANIMA
87.87.87

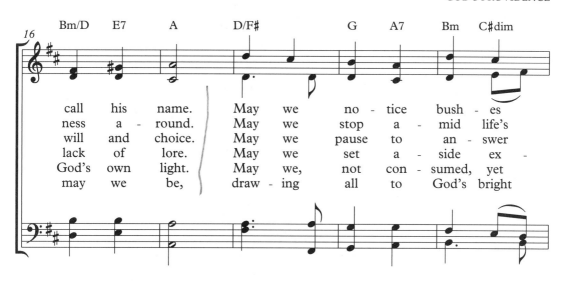

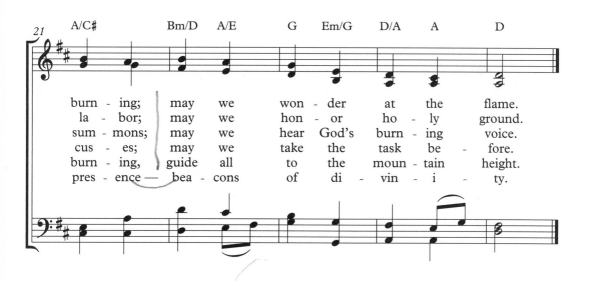

3030 Eternal God Transcending Time

Hvs.

-3

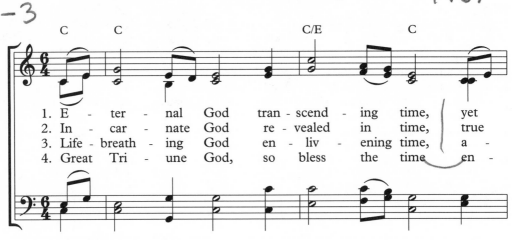

1. E - ter - nal God tran - scend - ing time, yet
2. In - car - nate God re - vealed in time, true
3. Life - breath - ing God en - liv - ening time, a -
4. Great Tri - une God, so bless the time en -

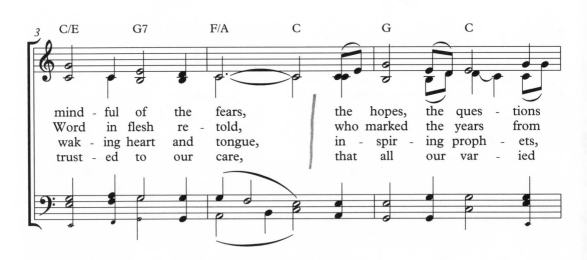

mind - ful of the fears, the hopes, the ques - tions
Word in flesh re - told, who marked the years from
wak - ing heart and tongue, in - spir - ing proph - ets,
trust - ed to our care, that all our var - ied

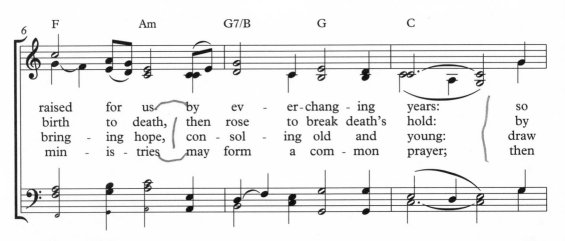

raised for us by ev - er - chang - ing years: so
birth to death, then rose to break death's hold: by
bring - ing hope, con - sol - ing old and young: draw
min - is - tries may form a com - mon prayer; then

WORDS: Carl P. Daw, Jr.
MUSIC: USA folk melody, Walker's *Southern Harmony*

RESIGNATION
CMD

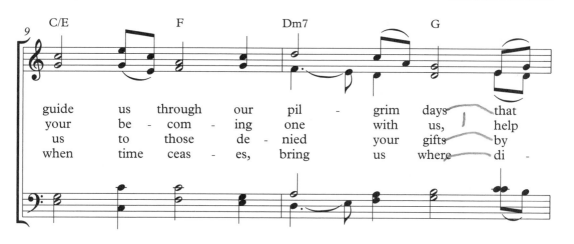

guide us through our pil - grim days that
your be - com - ing one with us, that help
us to those de - nied your gifts by
when time ceas - es, bring us where di -

we may find a home where jus - tice, truth, and
us to know and claim the u - ni - ty of
bi - as, want, or strife, con - vert our wills and
vi - sions are un - done, that in your pres - ence,

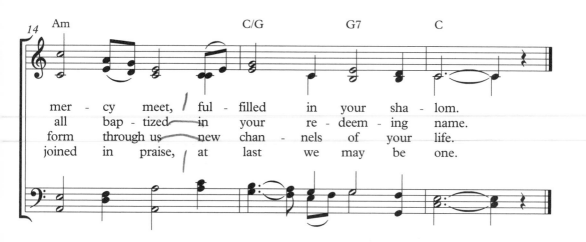

mer - cy meet, ful - filled in your sha - lom.
all bap - tized in your re - deem - ing name.
form through us new chan - nels of your life.
joined in praise, at last we may be one.

3031 God Leads Us Along

1. In shad-y, green pas-tures, so rich and so sweet, God
2. Some-times on the mount where the sun shines so bright, God
3. Though sor-rows be-fall us and e-vils op-pose, God

leads his dear chil-dren a-long; where the wa-ter's cool flow bathes the
leads his dear chil-dren a-long; some-times in the val-ley, in
leads his dear chil-dren a-long; through grace we can con-quer, de-

wea-ry one's feet, God leads his dear chil-dren a-long.
dark-est of night, God leads his dear chil-dren a-long.
feat all our foes, God leads his dear chil-dren a-long.

Refrain

Some through the wa-ters, some through the flood,

WORDS: G. A. Young
MUSIC: G. A. Young

GOD LEADS US
Irr. with Refrain

3032

Across the Lands

WORDS: Keith Getty and Stuart Townend
MUSIC: Keith Getty and Stuart Townend

ACROSS THE LANDS
87.87 D with Refrain

3033 God of Great and God of Small

1. God of great and God of small, God of one and
2. God of land and sky and sea, God of life and
3. God of si-lence, God of sound, God by whom the
4. God of heaven and God of earth, God of death and

God of all, God of weak and God of strong,
des-ti-ny, God of nev-er-end-ing power,
lost are found, God of day and dark-est night,
God of birth, God of now and days be-fore,

Refrain

God to whom all things be-long,
yet be-side me ev-ery hour, al-le-lu-ia,
God whose love turns wrong to right,
God who reigns for ev-er-more,

[1, 2, 3]
al-le-lu-ia, praise be to your name.
[4]
name.

WORDS: Natalie Sleeth
MUSIC: Natalie Sleeth

GOD OF GREAT AND SMALL
77.77 with Refrain

3034 God of Wonders

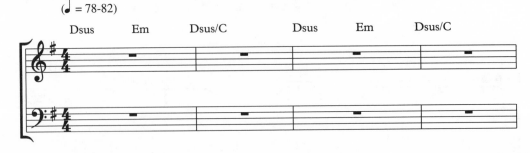

(♩ = 78-82)

Dsus Em Dsus/C Dsus Em Dsus/C

WORDS: Marc Byrd and Steve Hindalong
MUSIC: Marc Byrd and Steve Hindalong

GOD OF WONDERS
Irr. with Refrain

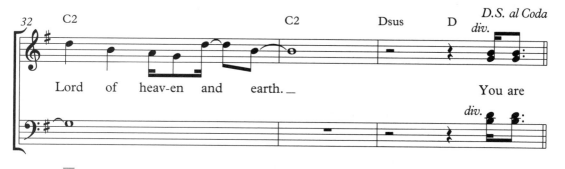

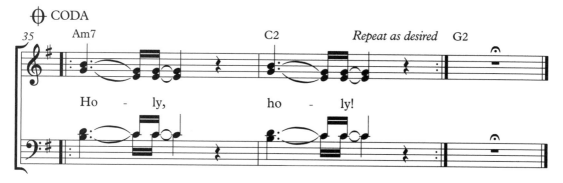

Bless Christ through Whom All Things Are Made 3035

1., 5. Bless Christ through whom all things are made. Join
2. Who makes the li - on and the lamb, the
3. Who made the ore for blood-soaked nails? Who
4. Who makes the wa - ters of our birth? Who

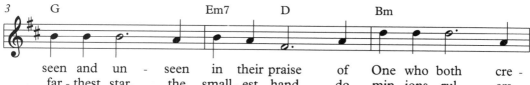

seen and un - seen in their praise of One who both cre -
far - thest star, the small - est hand, do - min - ions, rul - ers,
made the thorns and whip-ping tails? Who made the sun that
makes the dust where we re - turn? Who makes the way for

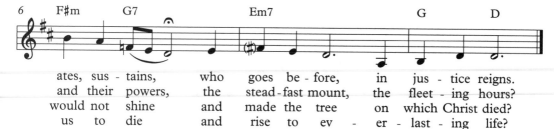

ates, sus - tains, who goes be - fore, in jus - tice reigns.
and their powers, the stead - fast mount, the fleet - ing hours?
would not shine and made the tree on which Christ died?
us to die and rise to ev - er - last - ing life?

WORDS: Lisa Ann Moss Degrenia (Col. 1:15-18)
MUSIC: Jim Strathdee

POXON
LM

3036 There's No One in This World Like Jesus

(Hakuna Wakaita sa Jesu)

There's no one in this world like Je - sus, there's
Ha - ku - na wa - kai - ta sa Je - su, ha -

no one in this world like him; there's no one in this world like
ku - na wa - kai - ta sa - ye; ha - ku - na wa - kai - ta sa

Je - sus, there's no one, there's no one like him.
Je - su, ha - ku, ha - ku - chi - na.

WORDS: Trad. Shona, Zimbabwe; English trans. by Patrick Matsikenyiri and
      Daniel Charles Damon
MUSIC: Trad. Shona, Zimbabwe, arr. by Patrick Matsikenyiri

HAKUNA WAKAITA
Irr.

3037

I Thank You, Jesus

WORDS: Kenneth Morris
MUSIC: Kenneth Morris, arr. by Joseph Joubert

Words and music © 1984 (renewed); arr. © 2006 Martin and Morris Studio, Inc., admin. by Unichappell Music

I THANK YOU
Irr.

3038

Mighty to Save

1. __ Ev-ery-one needs com-pas - sion, a love that's ne - ver fail-
2. So take me as you find__ me, __ all my fears and fail-

ing; let mer - cy fall on me. __ __ Ev-ery-one needs for-give-
ures; __ fill my life a - gain. __ I give my life to fol-

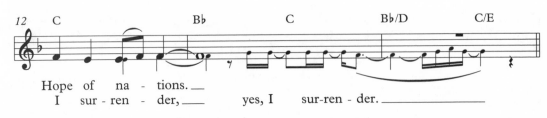

ness, the kind - ness of a Sav - ior, the
low __ ev-ery-thing I be - lieve __ in. Now

Hope of na - tions. __
I sur - ren - der, ___ yes, I sur - ren - der. _____

Refrain

Sav - ior, he can move the moun - tains; my God is

WORDS: Ben Fielding and Reuben Morgan
MUSIC: Ben Fielding and Reuben Morgan, arr. by Jay Rouse

MIGHTY TO SAVE
Irr.

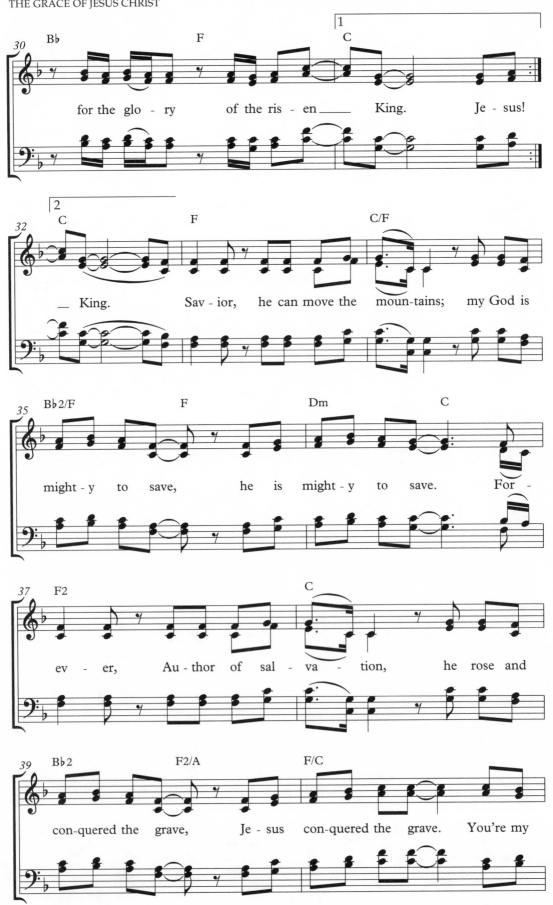

3039

Jesus, the Saving Name

WORDS: Timothy Dudley-Smith
MUSIC: Jane Marshall

TWENTY
SM

You Are My All in All

3040

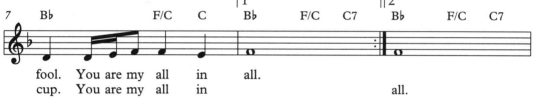

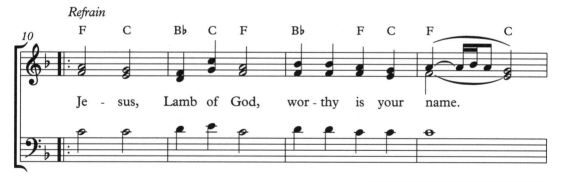

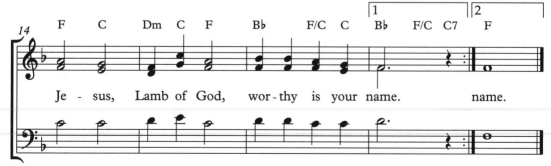

*Verses and refrain may be sung at the same time.

WORDS: Dennis Jernigan
MUSIC: Dennis Jernigan, arr. by William S. Moon

ALL IN ALL
885.885 with Refrain

3041

Praise Him

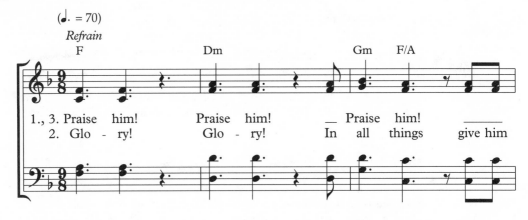

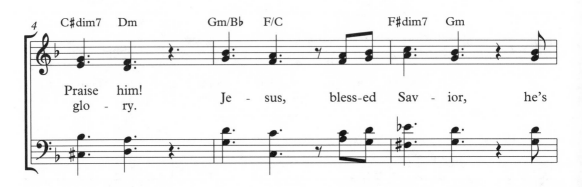

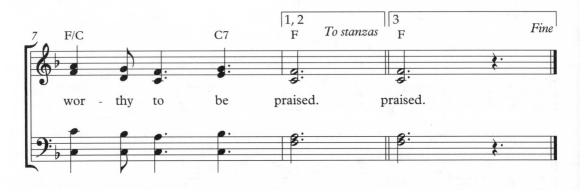

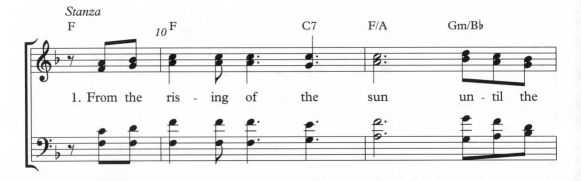

WORDS: Donnie Harper
MUSIC: Donnie Harper, arr. by Stephen Key

PRAISE HIM
Irr.

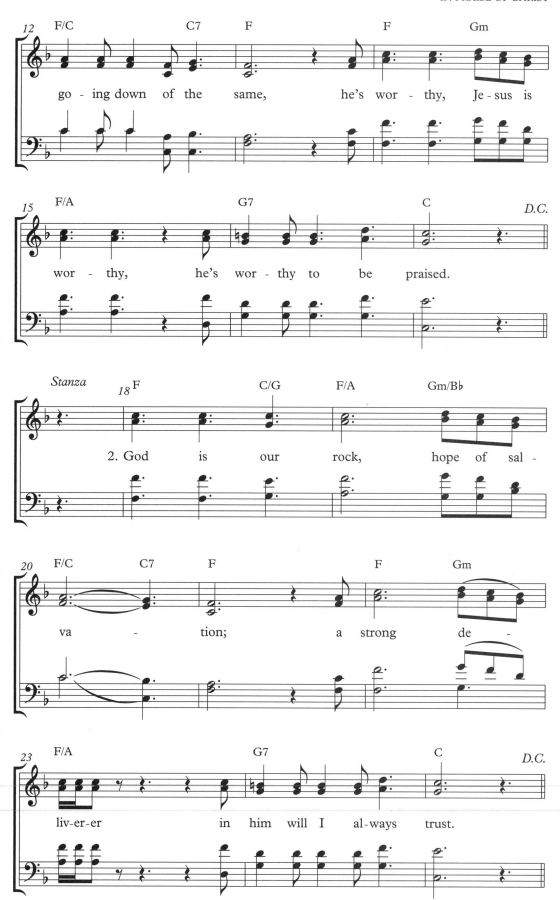

3042
Shout to the North

St. 1 - Men or All
St. 2 - Women or All
St. 3 - All

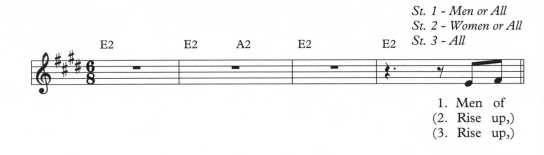

1. Men of
(2. Rise up,)
(3. Rise up,)

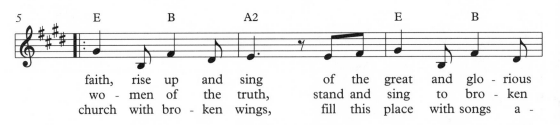

faith, rise up and sing of the great and glo-rious
wo-men of the truth, stand and sing to bro-ken
church with bro-ken wings, fill this place with songs a-

king. You are strong when you feel weak in your
hearts who can know the heal-ing power of our
gain of our God who reigns on high. By his

Third Time to Coda
(Final Refrain)

bro-ken-ness com-plete.
awe-some king of love.
grace a-gain we'll fly.

Refrain

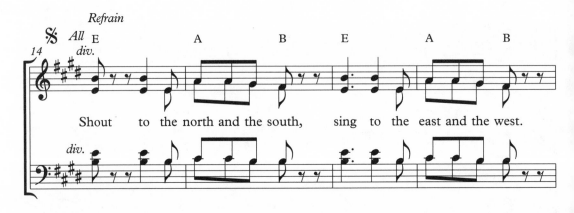

Shout to the north and the south, sing to the east and the west.

WORDS: Martin Smith
MUSIC: Martin Smith

SHOUT TO THE NORTH
Irr.

Play C#m7 and cue-size bass clef notes second time.

*Play C#m7 and cue-size bass clef notes second time.

You, Lord, Are Both Lamb and Shepherd 3043

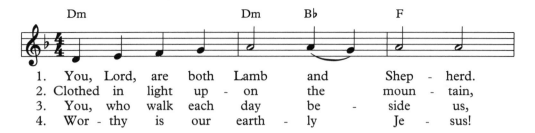

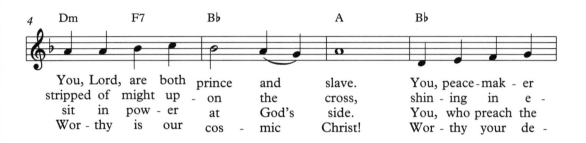

1. You, Lord, are both Lamb and Shep - herd.
2. Clothed in light up - on the moun - tain,
3. You, who walk each day be - side us,
4. Wor - thy is our earth - ly Je - sus!

You, Lord, are both prince and slave. You, peace-mak - er
stripped of might up - on the cross, shin - ing in e -
sit in pow - er at God's side. You, who preach the
Wor - thy is our cos - mic Christ! Wor - thy your de -

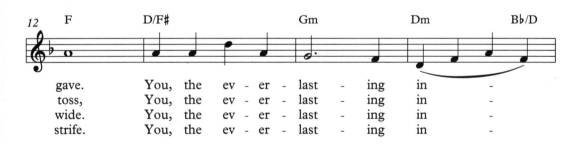

and sword - bring - er of the way you took and
ter - nal glo - ry, beg - gar'd by a sol - dier's
way that's nar - row, have a love that reach - es
feat and vic - tory. Wor - thy still your peace and

gave. You, the ev - er - last - ing in -
toss, You, the ev - er - last - ing in -
wide. You, the ev - er - last - ing in -
strife. You, the ev - er - last - ing in -

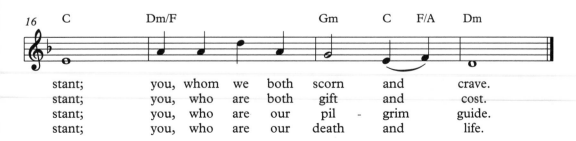

stant; you, whom we both scorn and crave.
stant; you, who are both gift and cost.
stant; you, who are our pil - grim guide.
stant; you, who are our death and life.

WORDS: Sylvia Dunstan
MUSIC: French Carol
Words © 1991 GIA Publications, Inc.

PICARDY
87.87.87

3044

Make Way, Make Way

1. Make way, make way, for Christ the King in splen - dor ar - rives.
2. He comes the bro - ken hearts to heal, the pris - oners to free.

Fling wide the gates and wel - come him in - to your lives.
The deaf shall hear, the lame shall dance, the blind shall see.

Refrain

Part 1

Make way, make way for the

Part 2

Make way, make way

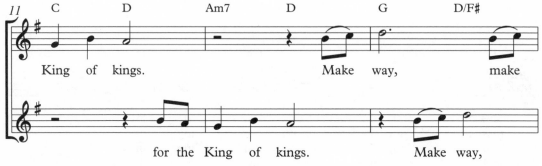

King of kings. Make way, make

for the King of kings. Make way,

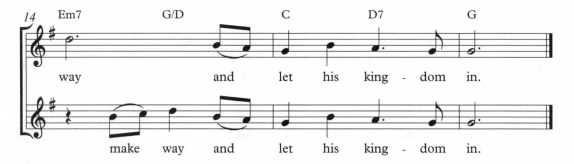

way and let his king - dom in.

make way and let his king - dom in.

WORDS: Graham Kendrick
MUSIC: Graham Kendrick; descant by Sharon Bradimore

MAKE WAY
86.84 with Refrain

4 vs. −1

Down by the Jordan

3045

1. Down by the Jordan, a proph-et named John was bap-tiz-ing, preach-ing a mes-sage the peo-ple found bold and sur-pris-ing. "God will for-give! Show that you'll change how you live! Sure-ly God's new day is ris-ing!"

2. There by the riv-er, the crowd came with great ex-pec-ta-tion: "Are you God's Cho-sen One, sent here to res-cue our na-tion?" "No!" John re-plied. "He who is might-ier than I judg-es and of-fers sal-va-tion."

3. Je-sus, you went to be bap-tized a-long with the oth-ers, tak-ing your place a-mong sin-ners, God's lost sons and daugh-ters. Then with great love, God's Spir-it came as a dove! Your work be-gan in those wa-ters.

4. Here in the Church, we are bap-tized and filled with God's Spir-it. Freed and for-giv-en we're wel-comed with joy! Can you hear it? This is God's sign! God says, "You're mine!" Let's take the good news and share it!

WORDS: Carolyn Winfrey Gillette
MUSIC: *Erneuerten Gesangbuch*, 1665; harm. by William Sterndale Bennett
Words © 2000 Carolyn Winfrey Gillette

LOBE DEN HERREN
14 14.478

3046 Come, O Redeemer, Come

1. Fa - ther, en-throned on high, ho - ly,
2. Lord, save us from the dark of our
3. Look now up - on our need, Lord, be

ho - ly; an - cient e - ter - nal Light, hear our prayer.
striv - ing, faith-less and trou-bled hearts, weighed
with us. Heal us and make us free from our

down.
sin.

Refrain

Come, O Re-deem-er, come, grant us

Last time to Coda ⊕   *D.S. al Coda*

mer-cy. Come, O Re-deem-er, come, grant us peace.

⊕ CODA

grant us peace.

WORDS: Fernando Ortega
MUSIC: Fernando Ortega

ORTEGA
64.63 with Refrain

© 1996 IzzySolSongs, admin. by Metro One

3047 God Almighty, We Are Waiting

1. God Al - might - y, we are wait - ing for a Sav - ior
2. God In - car - nate, we are wait - ing for the feast day
3. God the Spir - it, we are wait - ing for your pres - ence

WORDS: E. Ann Bell
MUSIC: Rowland H. Prichard; harm. from *The English Hymnal*, 1906
Words © 2005 Hope Publishing Company

HYFRYDOL
87.87 D

(USE: WOV #760)

3048 View the Present through the Promise

1. View the pres-ent through the prom-ise, Christ will come a-gain.
2. Probe the pres-ent with the prom-ise, Christ will come a-gain.
3. Match the pres-ent to the prom-ise, Christ will come a-gain.

Trust de-spite the deep-ening dark-ness, Christ will come a-gain.
Let your dai-ly ac-tions wit-ness, Christ will come a-gain.
Make this hope your guid-ing prem-ise, Christ will come a-gain.

Lift the world a-bove its griev-ing through your watch-ing and be-liev-ing
Let your lov-ing and your giv-ing and your jus-tice and for-giv-ing
Pat-tern all your cal-cu-lat-ing and the world you are cre-a-ting

in the hope past hope's con-ceiv-ing: Christ will come a-gain.
be a sign to all the liv-ing: Christ will come a-gain.
to the ad-vent you are wait-ing: Christ will come a-gain.

WORDS: Thomas H. Troeger
MUSIC: Trad. Welsh melody; harm. by Luther Orlando Emerson

AR HYD Y NOS (alt.)
85.85.888.5

3049

Wait for the Lord

Wait for the Lord, whose day is near.

Wait for the Lord: keep watch, take heart!

WORDS: Jacques Berthier (Ps. 27:14)
MUSIC: Jacques Berthier

WAIT FOR THE LORD
44.44

Stanzas *(superimposed on ostinato chorale)*

Leader   (Isaiah 40:3)

1. Pre-pare the way for the Lord. Make a straight path for God.

(Sing either part)

Pre - pare the way for the Lord.

(Phil. 4:4-5, Psalm 70:4)

2. Re-joice in the Lord al-ways: God is at hand.

Joy and glad-ness for all who seek the Lord.

MUSIC: Jacques Berthier

(Isaiah 40:5)

3. The glo-ry of the Lord shall be re- vealed. All the earth will see the Lord.

(Psalm 38:15)

4. I wait - ed for the Lord. God heard my cry.

(Psalm 123:2)

5. Our eyes are fixed on the Lord, our God.

(Matthew 6:33; 7:7)

6. Seek first the king-dom of God. Seek and you shall find.

(Psalm 86:11)

7. O Lord show us your way. Guide us in your truth.

3050

Until Jesus Comes

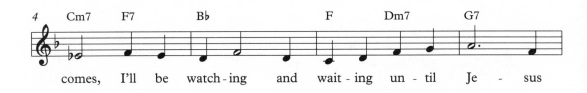

WORDS: Dean McIntyre
MUSIC: Dean McIntyre

PAROUSIA
55.75 D

A Star Shone Bright

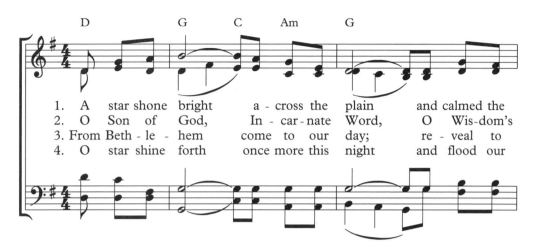

1. A star shone bright a-cross the plain and calmed the
2. O Son of God, In-car-nate Word, O Wis-dom's
3. From Beth-le-hem come to our day; re-veal to
4. O star shine forth once more this night and flood our

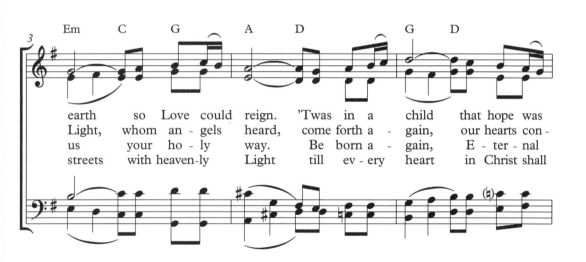

earth so Love could reign. 'Twas in a child that hope was
Light, whom an-gels heard, come forth a-gain, our hearts con-
us your ho-ly way. Be born a-gain, E-ter-nal
streets with heaven-ly Light till ev-ery heart in Christ shall

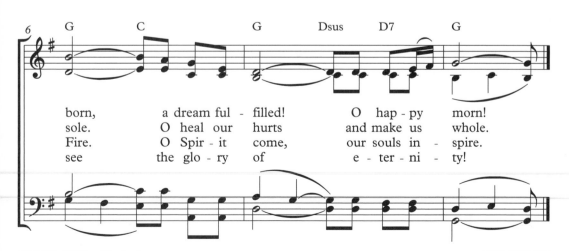

born, a dream ful-filled! O hap-py morn!
sole. O heal our hurts and make us whole.
Fire. O Spir-it come, our souls in-spire.
see the glo-ry of e-ter-ni-ty!

WORDS: F. Richard Garland
MUSIC: English folk melody; harm. by Dean McIntyre

O WALY WALY
LM

3052 God Rest You Merry, Gentlemen *(folk)

1. God rest you mer - ry, gen - tle-men, let noth-ing you dis - may,
2. In Beth - le - hem in Ju - dah this bless-ed babe was born,
3. From God our heaven-ly Fa - ther a bless-ed an - gel came,
4. The shep-herds at those tid - ings re - joic-ed much in mind,
5. Now to the Lord sing prais - es, all you with-in this place,

for Je - sus Christ our Sav - ior was born up - on this day,
and laid with - in a man - ger up - on this bless - ed morn:
and un - to cer - tain shep - herds brought tid-ings of the same,
and left their flocks a - feed - ing in tem-pest, storm, and wind,
and with true love and broth-er-hood each oth - er now em - brace;

to save us all from Sa - tan's power when we were gone a - stray.
for which his moth-er Ma - ry did noth-ing take in scorn.
how that in Beth - le - hem was born the Son of God by name.
and went to Beth - le - hem straight-way, the bless-ed babe to find.
this ho - ly tide of Christ - mas all oth - ers doth de - face.

Refrain

O tid - ings of com - fort and joy, com-fort and

WORDS: Trad. English carol, 18th cent.
MUSIC: Trad. English melody

GOD REST YOU MERRY
Irr. with Refrain

Bethlehem

3053

Fast (♩ = 142)

Refrain

joy; O tid - ings of com - fort and joy.

Beth - le - hem, ___ Beth - le - hem, ___
cit - y where ___ the King was born. ___ Beth - le - hem, ___
Beth - le - hem, ___ Ma - ry had - a Je - sus on Christ - mas morn. ___ *Fine*

Leader ... *All*

1. Ma - ry, Ma - ry, meek and mild; ___ Ma - ry had - a Je - sus on
2. Jo - seph took Ma - ry by the hand, ___ Ma - ry had - a Je - sus on
3. Ma - ry put Je - sus in the hay. ___ Ma - ry had - a Je - sus on

Leader

Christ - mas morn. ___ Moth - er of ___ the Ho - ly Child. ___
Christ - mas morn. ___ Trav - el - ing ___ through - out the land. ___
Christ - mas morn. ___ That was his bed ___ on Christ - mas Day. ___

All ... *D.C. al Fine*

___ Ma - ry had - a Je - sus on Christ - mas morn. ___
___ Ma - ry had - a Je - sus on Christ - mas morn. ___
___ Ma - ry had - a Je - sus on Christ - mas morn. ___

WORDS: Marilyn E. Thornton
MUSIC: Marilyn E. Thornton
© 1985 Marilyn E. Thornton

BETHLEHEM
Irr. with Refrain

3054

Chinese Lantern Carol

1. Ti - ny hand strike ti - ny chime! Chil-dren all in a row
2. Bow to gen - tle Ma - ry mild, bow to Jo - seph, so,
3. All your wor - ry, hun-ger, and pain be for - got-ten to - night;

jour - ney make at Christ-mas - time like so long a - go.
light my lan - tern for this child born so long a - go.
Je - sus born on Beth - le-hem plain so the world may be bright.

To the man - ger hur - ry to him, foot-steps o - ver the snow;
Would my Christ-mas lan - tern glow as the star did then,
God, from whom all bless - ings flow, chil - dren near and far,

1, 2

how to find small Beth - le - hem? Lan - tern star will show.
bring - ing peace to earth be - low, and good will to all.
make your lov - ing spir - it glow

3

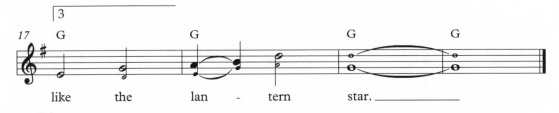

like the lan - tern star. _____

WORDS: Jacqueline Hanna McNair
MUSIC: Chinese folk melody; arr. by Jacqueline Hanna McNair

LANTERN STAR
Irr.

Come, Little Children

3055

1. Come, lit - tle chil - dren, to the si - lent man - ger.
2. Come, lit - tle chil - dren, to the lit - tle broth - er.
3. Come, lit - tle chil - dren, to the God of glo - ry.

Come, lit - tle chil - dren, see the mys - ter - y. Come, lit - tle chil - dren, to the
Come, lit - tle chil - dren, hear the ba - by cry. Come, lit - tle chil - dren, see the
Come, lit - tle chil - dren, see the Light of light. Come, lit - tle chil - dren, hear the

lit - tle stran - ger. Come, lit - tle chil - dren, to na - tiv - i - ty.
Ma - ry moth - er. Come, lit - tle chil - dren, see the star on high.
gos - pel sto - ry. Come, lit - tle chil - dren, it is Christ - mas night.

WORDS: Herbert F. Brokering, Robert Sterling, and Rusty Edwards
MUSIC: Herbert K. Brokering, Robert Sterling, and Rusty Edwards

HOWARD
11 10.11 10

3056 Jesus, the Light of the World

1. See the bright and Morn-ing Star, Je-sus, the Light of the World!
2. He's the lamp that lights our way, Je-sus, the Light of the World!
3. No more dark-ness, no more night — Je-sus, the Light of the World!

He has ris-en in our hearts, Je-sus, the Light of the World!
Step by step and day by day — Je-sus, the Light of the World!
He will shine for-ev-er bright, Je-sus, the Light of the World!

Refrain

Walk in the light, beau-ti-ful light; come where his love and his mer-cy are bright.

Shine all a-round us by day and by night, Je-sus, the Light of the World.

WORDS: Ken Bible and George D. Elderkin
MUSIC: George D. Elderkin; arr. by Ken Bible

ELDERKIN
77.77 with Refrain

Glory in the Highest

(*Gloria en las alturas*)

WORDS: Traditional Puerto Rican; English trans. by Gerhard Cartford
MUSIC: Traditional Puerto Rican; arr. by Raquel Mora Martínez

GLORIA
65.65 D

Trans. © 1998 Augsburg Fortress; arr. © 2004 Raquel Mora Martínez

3058

Mary Had a Baby

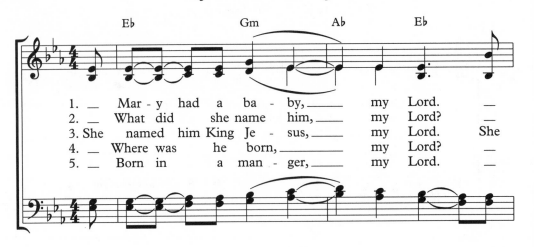

1. __ Mar-y had a ba-by, ____ my Lord. __
2. __ What did she name him, ____ my Lord? __
3. She named him King Je-sus, ____ my Lord. She
4. __ Where was he born, ____ my Lord? __
5. __ Born in a man-ger, ____ my Lord. __

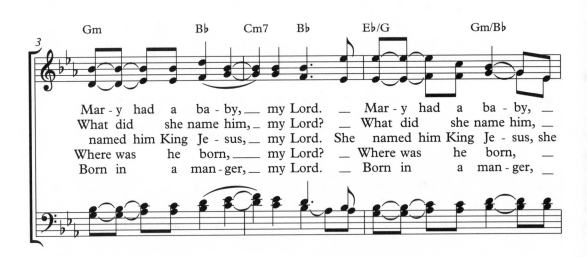

Mar-y had a ba-by, __ my Lord. __ Mar-y had a ba-by, __
What did she name him, __ my Lord? __ What did she name him, __
named him King Je-sus, __ my Lord. She named him King Je-sus, she
Where was he born, ____ my Lord? __ Where was he born, __
Born in a man-ger, __ my Lord. __ Born in a man-ger, __

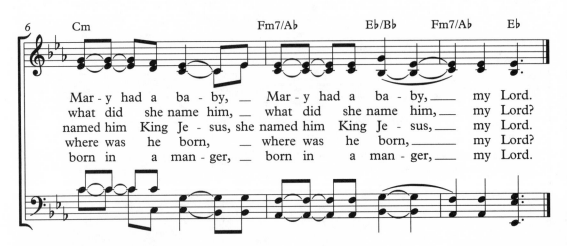

Mar-y had a ba-by, __ Mar-y had a ba-by, ____ my Lord.
what did she name him, __ what did she name him, __ my Lord?
named him King Je-sus, she named him King Je-sus, ____ my Lord.
where was he born, __ where was he born, ____ my Lord?
born in a man-ger, __ born in a man-ger, ____ my Lord.

WORDS: African American spiritual
MUSIC: African American spiritual; arr. by Kenneth L. Fenton

MARY HAD A BABY
Irr.

Love Has Come

3059

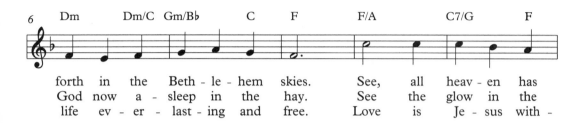

1. Love has come — a light in the dark - ness! Love shines
2. Love is born! Come, share in the won - der. Love is
3. Love has come and nev - er will leave us! Love is

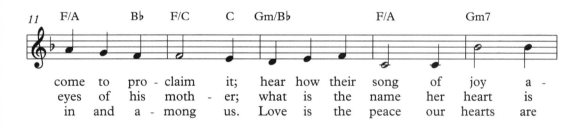

forth in the Beth - le - hem skies. See, all heav - en has
God now a - sleep in the hay. See the glow in the
life ev - er - last - ing and free. Love is Je - sus with -

come to pro - claim it; hear how their song of joy a -
eyes of his moth - er; what is the name her heart is
in and a - mong us. Love is the peace our hearts are

ris - es: Love! Love! Born un - to you, a Sav - ior!
say - ing? Love! Love! Love is the name she whis - pers.
seek - ing. Love! Love! Love is the gift of Christ - mas.

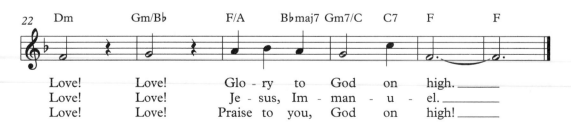

Love! Love! Glo - ry to God on high._____
Love! Love! Je - sus, Im - man - u - el._____
Love! Love! Praise to you, God on high!_____

WORDS: Ken Bible
MUSIC: Traditional French

BRING A TORCH
9.9.10 9.9.8

3060 Jesus, Jesus, Oh, What a Wonderful Child

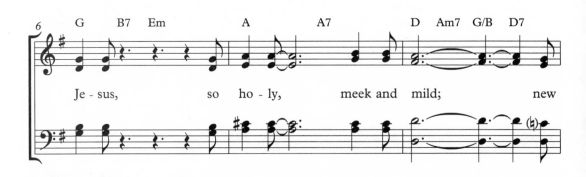

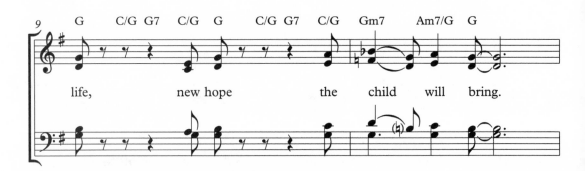

WORDS: Traditional African American
MUSIC: Traditional African American; vocal arr. by Jeffrey Radford
Vocal arr. © 1992 The Pilgrim Press

WONDERFUL CHILD
Irr.

Lis - ten to the an - gel sing, "Glo - ry, glo - ry,

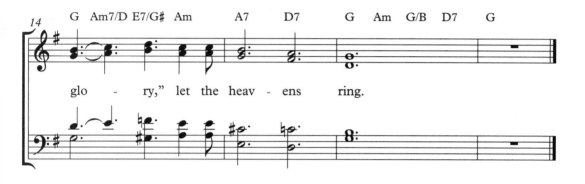

glo - ry," let the heav - ens ring.

3061 See Him Lying on a Bed of Straw

1. See him ly-ing on a bed of straw: a draft-y sta-ble with an o-pen door; Ma-ry cra-dl-ing the babe she bore — the Prince of glo-ry is his name.
2. Star of sil-ver, sweep a-cross the skies, — show where Je-sus in the man-ger lies; shep-herds, swift-ly from your stu-por rise to see the Sav-ior of the world!
3. An-gels, sing a-gain the song you sang, — sing the glo-ry of God's gra-cious plan; sing that Beth-lehem's lit-tle ba-by can — be the Sav-ior of us all.
4. Mine are rich-es, from your pov-er-ty, — from your in-no-cence, e-ter-ni-ty; mine, for-give-ness by your death for me, — Child of sor-row for my joy.

Refrain

Oh, now car-ry me to Beth-le-hem to see the Lord of love a-gain: just as poor as was the sta-ble then, the [1-3] Prince of glo-ry when he came. [4] sta-ble then, the Prince of glo-ry when he came.

WORDS: Michael Perry
MUSIC: Michael Perry; arr. by Stephen Coates

CALYPSO CAROL
Irr.

Spirit-Child Jesus

3062

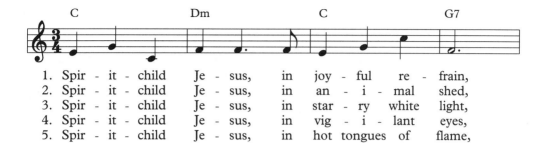

1. Spir - it - child Je - sus, in joy - ful re - frain,
2. Spir - it - child Je - sus, in an - i - mal shed,
3. Spir - it - child Je - sus, in star - ry white light,
4. Spir - it - child Je - sus, in vig - i - lant eyes,
5. Spir - it - child Je - sus, in hot tongues of flame,

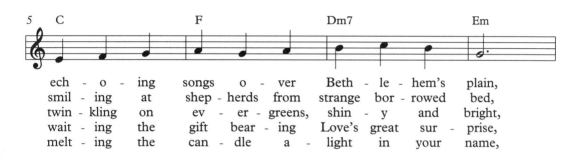

ech - o - ing songs o - ver Beth - le - hem's plain,
smil - ing at shep - herds from strange bor - rowed bed,
twin - kling on ev - er - greens, shin - y and bright,
wait - ing the gift bear - ing Love's great sur - prise,
melt - ing the can - dle a - light in your name,

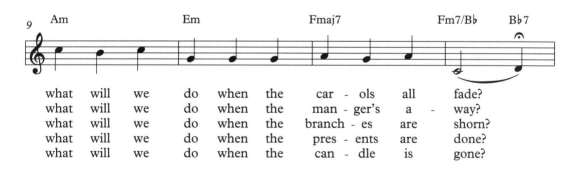

what will we do when the car - ols all fade?
what will we do when the man - ger's a - way?
what will we do when the branch - es are shorn?
what will we do when the pres - ents are done?
what will we do when the can - dle is gone?

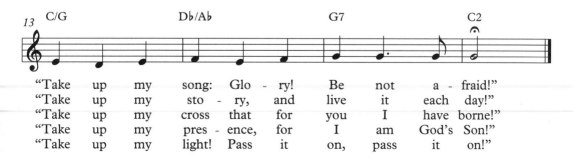

"Take up my song: Glo - ry! Be not a - fraid!"
"Take up my sto - ry, and live it each day!"
"Take up my cross that for you I have borne!"
"Take up my pres - ence, for I am God's Son!"
"Take up my light! Pass it on, pass it on!"

WORDS: Mary Nelson Keithahn
MUSIC: John D. Horman

SPIRIT-CHILD
10 10.10 10

3063   If I Could Visit Bethlehem

METRE: 8686 8686 (CMD)

G   Am/G   G   Dm7   Am7   G

1. If I could vis-it Beth-le-hem what pres-ents would I bring?
2. I'd learn some sim-ple word to speak in Ar-a-ma-ic tongues.
3. I'd say, "He'll nev-er hurt or kill, and joy will fol-low tears.

D   5 G   Am/G   G   Am   Dsus   D

If I could see what hap-pened then, what would I say or sing?
I'd cra-dle him, and kiss his cheek, and say, "I'm glad you've come."
We'll know his name and love him still in twen-ty hun-dred years."

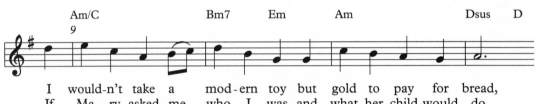

Am/C   Bm7   Em   Am   Dsus   D

I would-n't take a mod-ern toy but gold to pay for bread,
If Ma-ry asked me who I was and what her child would do,
I can-not vis-it Beth-le-hem but what I can, I'll do:

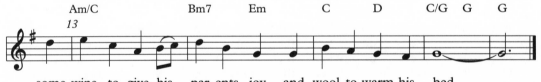

Am/C   Bm7   Em   C   D   C/G   G   G

some wine to give his par-ents joy and wool to warm his bed. _____
I would-n't talk a-bout the cross or tell her all I knew. _____
I'll love you, Je-sus, as my friend, and give my life to you. _____

WORDS: Brian Wren
MUSIC: Hal H. Hopson

CAROL STREAM
CMD

On Christmas Night

3064

METRE: 8888/88

1. On Christ-mas night all Chris-tians sing, to hear the news the
2. Then why should we on earth be sad, since our Re-deem-er
3. When sin de-parts be-fore his grace, then life and health come
4. All out of dark-ness we have light, which made the an - gels

an - gels bring. On Christ - mas night all Chris - tians sing, to
made us glad. Then why should we on earth be sad, since
in its place. When sin de - parts be - fore his grace, then
sing this night. All out of dark - ness we have light, which

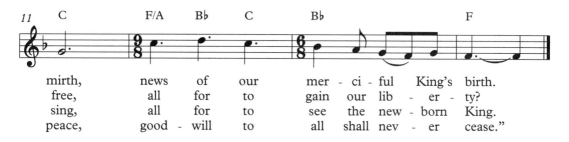

hear the news the an - gels bring: news of great joy, news of great
our Re - deem - er made us glad; when from our sin he set us
life and health come in its place; heav - en and earth with joy may
made the an - gels sing this night: "Glo - ry to God, on earth be

mirth, news of our mer - ci - ful King's birth.
free, all for to gain our lib - er - ty?
sing, all for to see the new - born King.
peace, good - will to all shall nev - er cease."

WORDS: Traditional English
MUSIC: Traditional English melody

SUSSEX CAROL
LM

3065 Some Children See Him

1. Some chil-dren see him lil-y white, the baby Jesus born this night, some children see him lil-y white, with tress-es soft and fair.

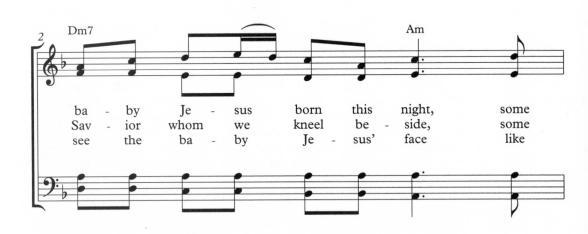

2. Some chil-dren see him al-mond-eyed, this Savior whom we kneel be-side, some children see him al-mond-eyed, with skin of yel-low hue.

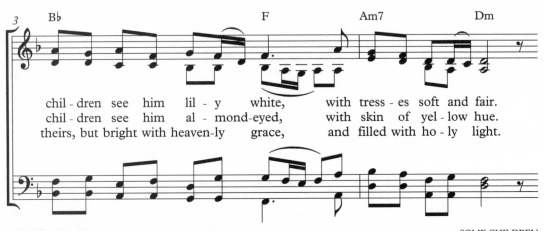

3. The chil-dren in each dif-ferent place will see the ba-by Je-sus' face like theirs, but bright with heaven-ly grace, and filled with ho-ly light.

WORDS: Wihla Hutson
MUSIC: Alfred Burt

SOME CHILDREN
86.86 D

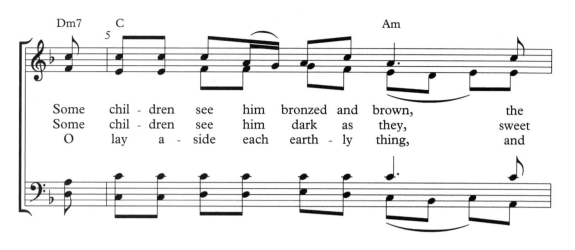

Some chil - dren see him bronzed and brown, the
Some chil - dren see him dark as they, sweet
O lay a - side each earth - ly thing, and

Lord of heaven to earth come down; some
Ma - ry's Son to whom we pray; some
with thy heart as of - fer - ing, come

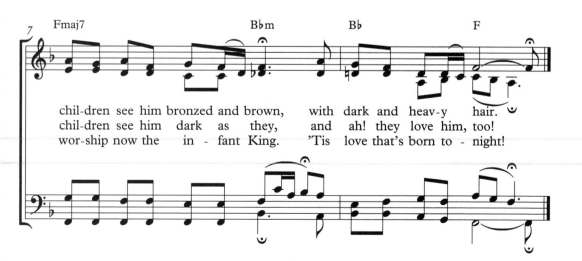

chil - dren see him bronzed and brown, with dark and heav-y hair.
chil - dren see him dark as they, and ah! they love him, too!
wor - ship now the in - fant King. 'Tis love that's born to - night!

3066

Still, Still, Still

WORDS: Traditional Austrian carol
MUSIC: Melody from *Salzburger Volkslieder*; arr. by Dean McIntyre

STILL, STILL, STILL
99.89

This page blank to facilitate page turns

3067 Welcome to Our World

With feeling (♩ = 84)

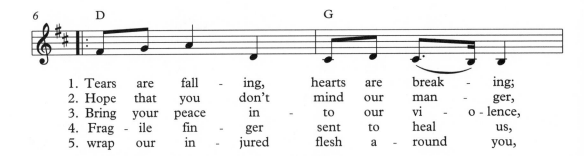

1. Tears are fall - ing, hearts are break - ing;
2. Hope that you don't mind our man - ger,
3. Bring your peace in - to our vi - o - lence,
4. Frag - ile fin - ger sent to heal us,
5. wrap our in - jured flesh a - round you,

how we need to hear from God. __ You've been prom - ised,
how I wish we would have known. but long a - wait - ed
bid our hun - gry souls be filled. __ Word now break - ing
ten - der brow pre - pared for thorn, __ ti - ny heart whose
breathe our air and walk our sod. __ Rob our sin and

we've been wait - ing, wel - come ho - ly Child, __ __
ho - ly stran - ger, make your - self at home, __ please
heav - en's si - lence, wel - come to our world, __ __
blood will save us, un - to us is born, __ __
make us ho - ly, per - fect Son of God, __ __

1-4 (2)

wel - come ho - ly Child. _____ 2. __
make your-self at home. _____ 3. __
wel - come to our world. _____ 4. __
un - to us is born. _____ 5. So

WORDS: Chris Rice
MUSIC: Chris Rice

WELCOME TO OUR WORLD
Irr.

3068

The Lord's Prayer

WORDS: Based on Matt. 6:9-13
MUSIC: Albert Malotte, arr. by Richard Huggins

MALOTTE
Irr.

The Lord's Prayer
(Padre nuestro)

WORDS: Based on Matt. 6:9-13; Spanish trans. by Carlos Rosas;
       English adapt. by Dean McIntyre
MUSIC: Carlos Rosas

PADRE NUESTRO
Irr. with Refrain

Spanish trans. and music © 1976 Oregon Catholic Press; English adaptation © 2001 The General Board of Discipleship
of The United Methodist Church

The Lord's Prayer

WORDS: Based on Matt. 6:9-13
MUSIC: David Haas

Music © 1986 GIA Publications

LORD'S PRAYER (HAAS)
Irr.

The Lord's Prayer

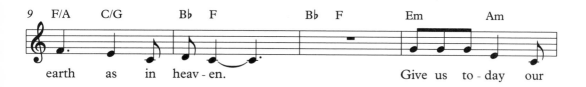

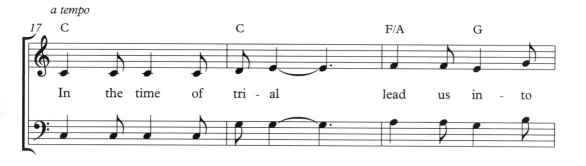

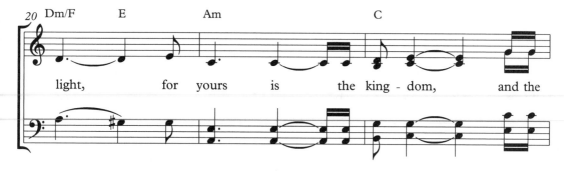

WORDS: Matt. 6:9-13, adapt. by Mark A. Miller and Laurie Zelman
MUSIC: Mark A. Miller

LORD'S PRAYER (MILLER)
Irr.

pow - er,   and the glo - ry,   for - ev -

er.   Our   God,   in

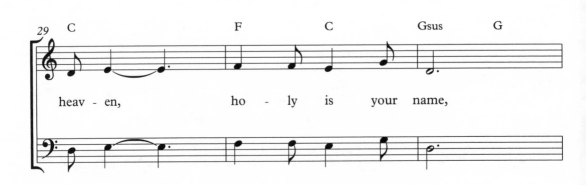

heav - en,   ho - ly is   your name,

ho - ly is   your   name.

Cast Out, O Christ

1. Cast out, O Christ, cast far a - way the
2. Our rag - ing griefs, our jeal - ous fears are
3. Once long a - go, from Gal - i - lee, you
4. Your Word breathes life and health and hope that
5. So come, O Christ and cast a - way the

de - mons that de - stroy: the haunt - ing dreads that
Le - gion in their name. Our shack - led hearts im -
sailed to storm - tossed shores. And still, in power, you
break through e - vil's thrall. You send us, strength - ened,
de - mons that de - stroy. Trans - form our lives to

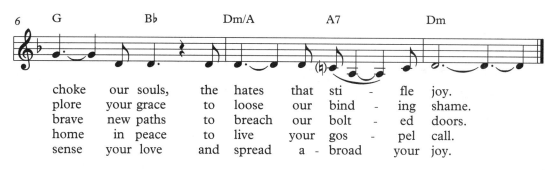

choke our souls, the hates that sti - fle joy.
plore your grace to loose our bind - ing shame.
brave new paths to breach our bolt - ed doors.
home in peace to live your gos - pel call.
sense your love and spread a - broad your joy.

WORDS: Mary Louise Bringle
MUSIC: American folk melody; arr. by Dean McIntyre, alt.

HOUSE OF THE RISING SUN
CM

3073

We Walk His Way

WORDS: South African; trans. by Anders Nyberg and Sven-Bernhard Fast

MUSIC: South African; arr. by Anders Nyberg

EWE THINA

Irr. with Refrain

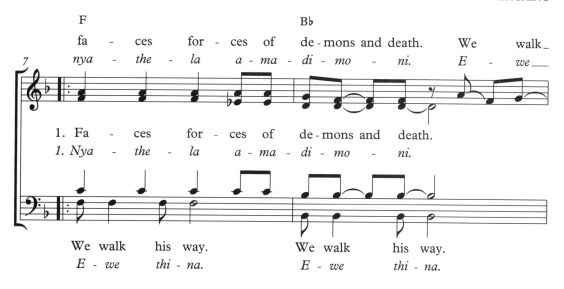

F   Bb

fa - ces for - ces of de-mons and death. We walk
nya - the - la a - ma - di - mo - ni. E - we

1. Fa - ces for - ces of de-mons and death.
1. Nya - the - la a - ma - di - mo - ni.

We walk his way.
E - we thi - na.

We walk his way.
E - we thi - na.

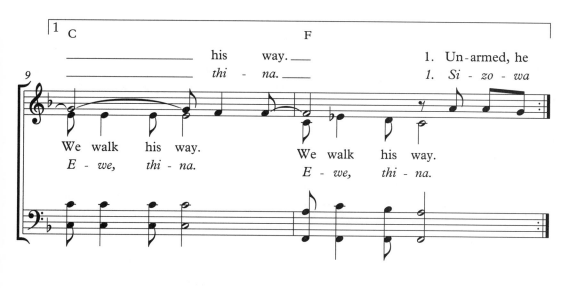

1. C   F

_____ his way. ___   1. Un-armed, he
_____ thi - na. ___   1. Si - zo - wa

We walk his way.
E - we, thi - na.

We walk his way.
E - we, thi - na.

2. C   F   *D.S. al Fine*

_____ his way. ___   We walk
_____ thi - na. ___   E - we

We walk his way.
E - we, thi - na.

We walk his way.
E - we, thi - na.

2. He breaks the bonds of hell dying on the cross,...

3. The tree of freedom blooms by his empty grave,...

3074 Jesus Is a Rock in a Weary Land

WORDS: African American spiritual
MUSIC: African American spiritual; arr. by Wyatt Tee Walker

WEARY LAND
Irr. with Refrain

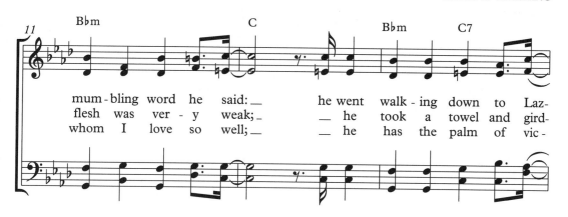

mum - bling word he said: ___ he went walk - ing down to Laz-
flesh was ver - y weak; ___ ___ he took a towel and gird-
whom I love so well; ___ ___ he has the palm of vic -

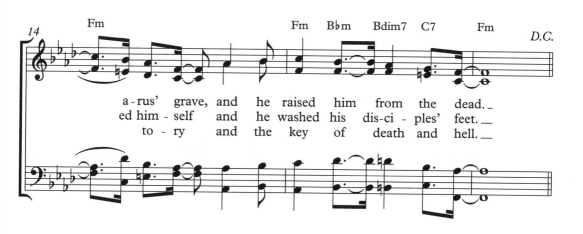

a - rus' grave, and he raised him from the dead. _
ed him - self and he washed his dis - ci - ples' feet. _
to - ry and the key of death and hell. _

Glory in the Cross

1. Let us ev-er glo-ry in the cross of Christ who re-
(2. Let us) bring our bur-dens to the cross of Christ who has
(3. Let us) kneel in hom-age at the cross of Christ where we

deems us with his blood. Let us tell the sto-ry of the
known our sor-row and tears. In the great com-pas-sion of the
see God's hu-man face. We be-hold the Mak-er of the

cross of Christ and the power of his sav - ing
heart of Christ, God has walked in our hopes and
sun and stars as he hangs on the throne of

WORDS: Dan Schutte
MUSIC: Dan Schutte
© 2000 Daniel L. Schutte

TRIDUUM
11 8.11 8 D

3076

Ivory Palaces

1. My Lord has gar - ments so won - drous fine, and myrrh their tex - ture fills; its fra - grance reached to this heart of mine, with joy my be - ing thrills.
2. His life had al - so its sor - rows sore, for al - oes had a part; and when I think of the cross he bore, my eyes with tear - drops start.
3. His gar - ments, too, were in cas - sia dipped, with heal - ing in a touch; each time my feet in some sin have slipped, he took me from its clutch.
4. In gar - ments glo - ri - ous he will come, to o - pen wide the door; and I shall en - ter my heaven - ly home, to dwell for - ev - er - more.

Refrain

(mel.) Out of the i - vo - ry pal - a - ces

WORDS: Henry Barraclough
MUSIC: Henry Barraclough

IVORY PALACES
96.96 with Refrain

into a world of woe, only his great e-
ternal love made my Savior go.

Blessed Is He Who Comes in God's Name 3077

1. "Bless-ed is he who comes in God's name!"
2. As the great cit-y came in-to view
3. They did not hear him; nei-ther do we.
4. Peace is not gained through pos-ture and threat.

cried the ex-cit-ed crowd. Spread-ing their cloaks, they
Je-sus be-gan to cry. "Would that you knew the
Might is our gold-en calf. We would see Christ e-
Jus-tice is not a game. Come, Chris-tians, turn; sur-

wel-comed a King; "Peace," they said, "here and now!"
mak-ings of peace!" he ut-tered with a sigh.
quipped with a sword, not with a shep-herd's staff.
ren-der the pride; re-pent in Je-sus' name.

WORDS: John Thornburg (Luke 19:28-47)
MUSIC: Jane Marshall

LAMENT
96.96

3078

Hosanna

WORDS: Mark 11:9
MUSIC: Patrick Roaché; arr. by Evelyn Simpson-Currenton

ROACHÉ
Irr.

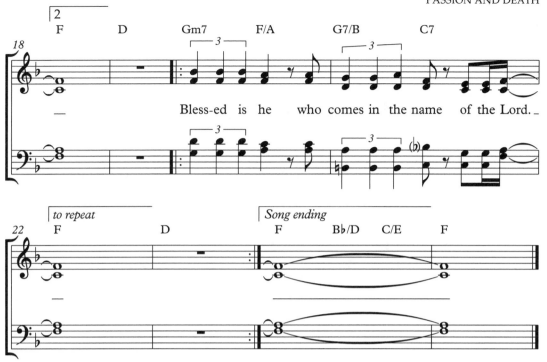

Blessed is he who comes in the name of the Lord.

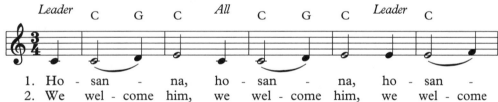

to repeat Song ending

Hosanna 3079

1. Ho - san - na, ho - san - na, ho - san -
2. We wel - come him, we wel - come him, we wel - come
3. We'll fol - low him, we'll fol - low him, we'll fol - low
4. We'll walk with him, we'll walk with him to Cal - va -
5. On Eas - ter morn, on Eas - ter morn we'll share the

na, ho - san - na.
him, we wel - come him.
him, we'll fol - low him. Ho - san - na, ho - san -
ry, to Cal - va - ry.
news, we'll share the news.

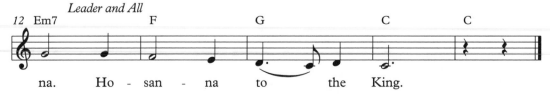

na. Ho - san - na to the King.

WORDS: Jim Strathdee
MUSIC: Jim Strathdee
© 1993 Desert Flower Music

STRATHDEE HOSANNA
Irr.

3080

Lord, Is It I?

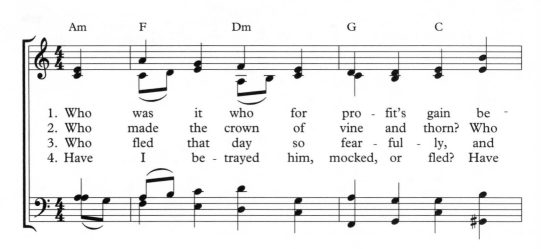

1. Who was it who for pro - fit's gain be -
2. Who made the crown of vine and thorn? Who
3. Who fled that day so fear - ful - ly, and
4. Have I be - trayed him, mocked, or fled? Have

trayed with fond em - brace the Lamb of God to
placed it on his brow? Whose an - gry words of
who de - nied their Lord? Who chose Ba - rab - bas
I my Lord de - nied? The cross is raised, but

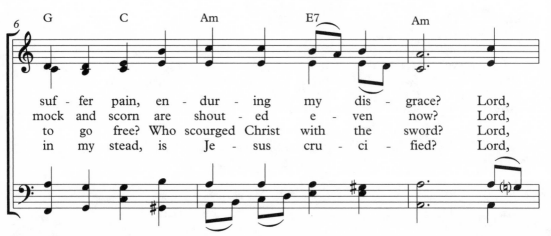

suf - fer pain, en - dur - ing my dis - grace? Lord,
mock and scorn are shout - ed e - ven now? Lord,
to go free? Who scourged Christ with the sword? Lord,
in my stead, is Je - sus cru - ci - fied? Lord,

WORDS: Dean McIntyre
MUSIC: Hans L. Hassler; harm. J. S. Bach

PASSION CHORALE
CMD

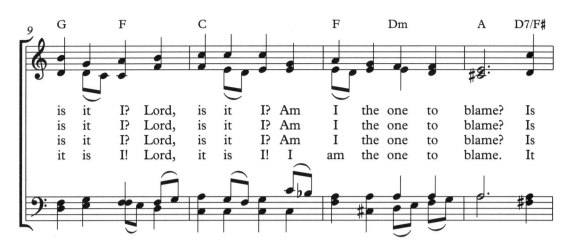

3081 Now Behold the Lamb

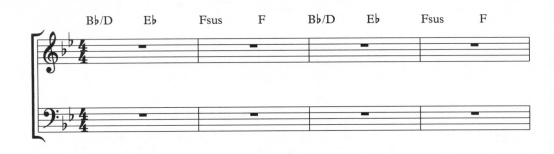

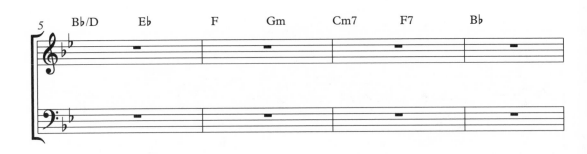

1. Now be-hold the Lamb, the pre-cious Lamb of God,
2. Ho - ly is the Lamb, the pre-cious Lamb of God.
3. Thank you for the Lamb, the pre-cious Lamb of God.

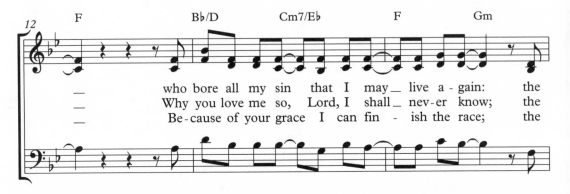

who bore all my sin that I may live a-gain: the
Why you love me so, Lord, I shall nev-er know; the
Be-cause of your grace I can fin - ish the race; the

WORDS: Kirk Franklin
MUSIC: Kirk Franklin

NOW BEHOLD THE LAMB
56.56.6

Cm7   Fsus   Bb   *D.S. al Coda*

You are the pre-cious Lamb of God.

⊕ CODA

Bb   Bb/D   *Leader or Solo*   Eb

3. E - ven when I broke Your

Fsus   F   Bb/D   Eb

heart, it was my sins that

Fsus   F   Bb/D   Eb

tore us a - part. But, I'm stand-ing right here

F   Gm   Cm7   Eb/F

in the midst of my tears. I claim You to be the Lamb of

to Verse 3 and Regular Ending

Bb   *All*   Bb/D   Fsus/Eb   F

God. Thank you for the Lamb, _ the

pre - cious Lamb of God. _ Be - cause of your grace I can fin-

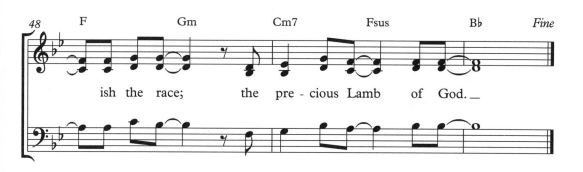

ish the race; the pre - cious Lamb of God. _

to Modulation and Song Ending

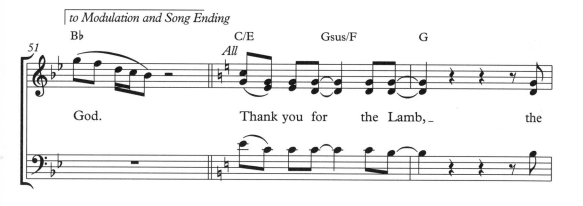

God. Thank you for the Lamb, _ the

pre - cious Lamb of God. _ Be - cause of your grace I can fin-

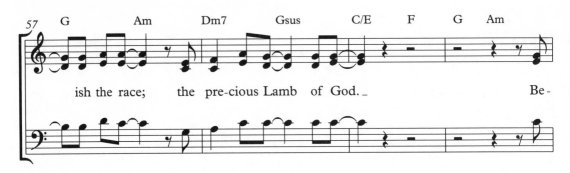

ish the race; the pre-cious Lamb of God. ___ Be-

cause of your grace I can fin - ish the race; the pre-cious Lamb of God. ___

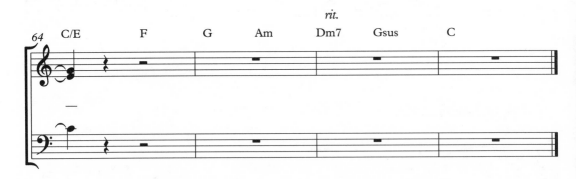

3082   Who Is He

1. Who is he who comes in tri - umph? Who is he who
2. See him there in hum - ble splen - dor. Hear them shout - ing
3. Rise and join the glad pro - ces - sion! Hear them pass - ing

WORDS: Ken Bible
MUSIC: Ludwig van Beethoven; arr. by Edward Hodges

HYMN TO JOY
87.87 D

SAME IN ALL EDITIONS!

3083   We Adore You, Jesus Christ
(Adoramus te Christe)

1 VS. ENG.
1 VS. LATIN

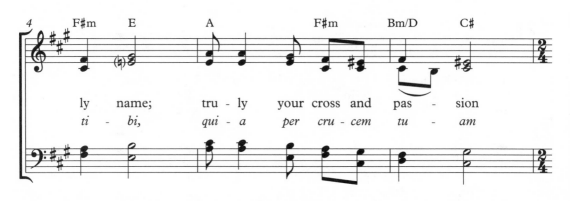

WORDS: Jacques Berthier
MUSIC: Jacques Berthier

ADORAMUS TE
77.76.76

O Christ, You Hang upon a Cross   3084

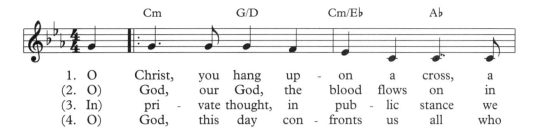

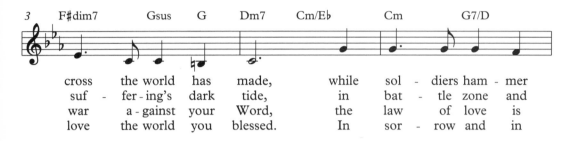

1. O   Christ,   you hang   up - on   a   cross,   a
(2. O)   God,   our God,   the   blood flows   on   in
(3. In)   pri - vate thought, in   pub - lic stance   we
(4. O)   God,   this day con - fronts us   all   who

cross   the world has   made,   while   sol - diers ham - mer
suf - fer - ing's dark tide,   in   bat - tle zone   and
war   a - gainst   your Word,   the   law   of love   is
love   the world   you   blessed.   In   sor - row and   in

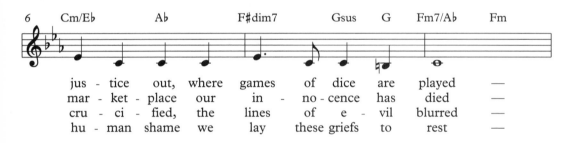

jus - tice out, where games of dice   are played   —
mar - ket - place our   in - no - cence has died   —
cru - ci - fied,   the   lines of e - vil blurred   —
hu - man shame   we   lay   these griefs to rest   —

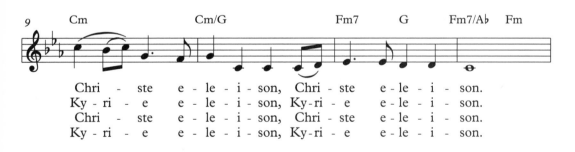

Chri - ste e - le - i - son, Chri - ste e - le - i - son.
Ky - ri - e e - le - i - son, Ky - ri - e e - le - i - son.
Chri - ste e - le - i - son, Chri - ste e - le - i - son.
Ky - ri - e e - le - i - son, Ky - ri - e e - le - i - son.

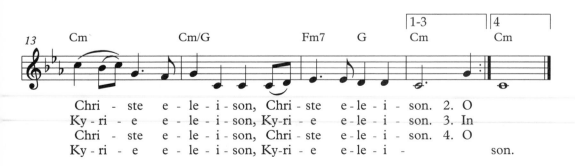

Chri - ste e - le - i - son, Chri - ste e - le - i - son. 2. O
Ky - ri - e e - le - i - son, Ky - ri - e e - le - i - son. 3. In
Chri - ste e - le - i - son, Chri - ste e - le - i - son. 4. O
Ky - ri - e e - le - i - son, Ky - ri - e e - le - i -   son.

WORDS: Shirley Erena Murray
MUSIC: Colin Gibson

GOOD FRIDAY
86.86.66.66

3085 The Power of the Cross

WORDS: Keith Getty and Stuart Townend
MUSIC: Keith Getty and Stuart Townend; choral parts arr. by Jeff Anderson

POWER OF THE CROSS
10 8.10 8.12 14

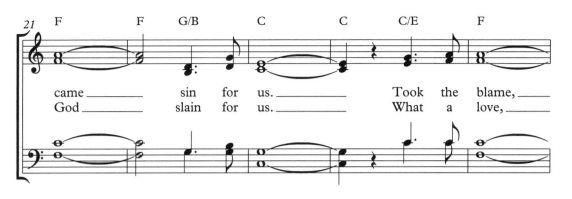

came _____ sin for us. _____ Took the blame, _____
God _____ slain for us. _____ What a love, _____

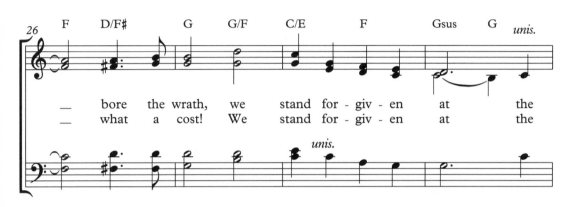

_ bore the wrath, we stand for - giv - en at the
_ what a cost! We stand for - giv - en at the

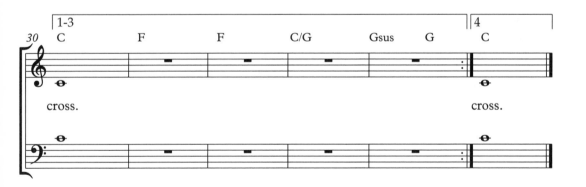

cross.   cross.

3086 Day of Arising

C   Am   Dm   G   F   C

1. Day of a - ris - ing, Christ on the road - way,
2. When we are walk - ing, doubt - ful and dread - ing,
3. "Lo, I am with you," Je - sus has spo - ken.
4. Christ our com - pan - ion, hope for the jour - ney,

7 Am   Em/G   F   C/E   Dm   G

un - known com - pan - ion walks with his own._____
blind - ed by sad - ness, slow - ness of heart,_____
This is Christ's prom - ise, this is Christ's sign:_____
bread of com - pas - sion, o - pen our eyes._____

13 C   F   F   C   Am   Dm/F

When they in - vite him, as fades the first day,
yet Christ walks with us ev - er a - wait - ing
when the church gath - ers, when bread is bro - ken,
Grant us your vi - sion, set all hearts burn - ing

19 D7/F#   C/G   F   G7   C   C

and bread is bro - ken, Christ is made known._____
our in - vi - ta - tion: Stay, do not part._____
there Christ is with us in bread and wine._____
that all cre - a - tion with you may rise._____

WORDS: Susan Palo Cherwien
MUSIC: Gaelic melody; harm. by Carlton R. Young

BUNESSAN
55.54 D

Words © 1996 Susan Palo Cherwien, admin. Augsburg Fortress; harm. © 1989 The United Methodist Publishing House, admin. by The Copyright Company

3087 O Christ, When You Ascended

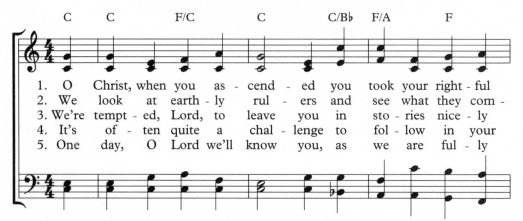

C   C   F/C   C   C/Bb   F/A   F

1. O Christ, when you as - cend - ed you took your right - ful
2. We look at earth - ly rul - ers and see what they com -
3. We're tempt - ed, Lord, to leave you in sto - ries nice - ly
4. It's of - ten quite a chal - lenge to fol - low in your
5. One day, O Lord we'll know you, as we are ful - ly

WORDS: Carolyn Winfrey Gillette
MUSIC: Henry T. Smart

LANCASHIRE
76.76 D

Words © 2007 Carolyn Winfrey Gillette

3088

Easter Alleluia

Al-le-lu-ia, al-le-lu-ia, al-le-lu - ia! _____

1. Glo - ry to God who does won - drous things,
2. See how sal - va - tion for all has been won,
3. Now in our pres - ence the Lord will ap - pear,
4. Call us, Good Shep - herd, we lis - ten for you,
5. Lord, we are o - pen to all that you say,
6. If we have love, then we dwell in the Lord,

let all the peo - ple God's prais - es now sing, all of cre - a - tion in
up from the grave our new life has be - gun, life now per - fect - ed in
shine in the fa - ces of all of us here, fill us with joy and cast
want - ing to see you in all that we do, we would the gate of sal -
read - y to lis - ten and fol - low your way, you are the pot - ter and
God will pro - tect us from fire and sword, fill us with love and the

splen-dor shall ring:
Je - sus the Son:
out all our fear: Al - le - lu - ia! _____
va - tion pass through:
we are the clay:
peace of his word:

WORDS: Marty Haugen
MUSIC: 15th cent. French carol; adapt. by Marty Haugen
Words and adapt. © 1986 GIA Publications, Inc.

O FILII ET FILIAE
10 10 10 with Alleluias

O Living God

3089

1. O liv-ing God, I long to see you lift-ed up in all your
2. O liv-ing God, I long to praise you heart and voice, with all cre-
3. O liv-ing God, I soon will see you face to face, in all your

glo - ry; to see you there in ho - ly beau - ty. O
a - tion; to wor-ship you for ten-der mer - cy. O
glo - ry. I'll wor-ship you in end-less won - der. O

Lord, al-might-y God, liv-ing Christ, I love you.
Lord, al-might-y God, liv-ing Christ, I love you.
Lord, al-might-y God, liv-ing Christ, I love you.

WORDS: Ken Bible
MUSIC: Traditional USA folk tune; arr. by Ken Bible
Words and arr. © 2000 LNWhymns.com, admin. by The Copyright Company

SHENANDOAH
989.66

The Easter Song

1. Hear the bells ring-ing, they're sing-ing that we can be born a-gain! The
2. Hear the bells ring-ing, they're sing-ing, "Christ is ris-en from the dead!"

an-gel up-on the tomb-stone said, "He is ris-en just as he said. Quick-ly now go tell his dis-

WORDS: Anne Herring
MUSIC: Anne Herring

EASTER SONG
Irr.

3091

Come, Holy Spirit

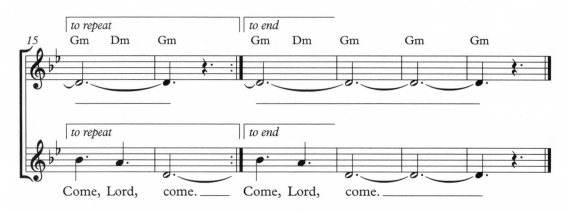

*Maranatha means "Come, soon."

WORDS: The Iona Community
MUSIC: The Iona Community

IONA MARANATHA
55.43

Come, Holy Spirit

3092

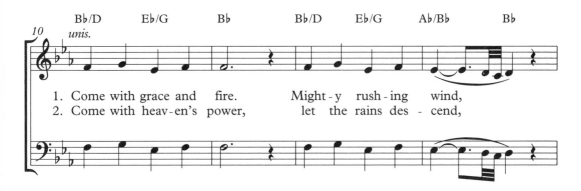

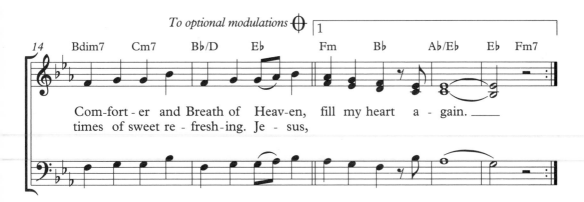

WORDS: Israel Houghton
MUSIC: Israel Houghton

COME, HOLY SPIRIT
Irr.

3093 Fill My Cup, Lord

1. Like the wom-an at the well I was seek-ing for things that could not sat-is-fy; and then I heard my Sav-ior speak-ing: "Draw from my well that nev-er shall run dry."

2. There are mil-lions in this world who are crav-ing the pleas-ure earth-ly things af-ford; but none can match the won-drous treas-ure that I find in Je-sus Christ my Lord.

3. So, my neigh-bor, if the things this world gave you leave you, if you kneel to him and hum-bly pray:

Refrain

Fill my cup, Lord, I lift it up, Lord! Come and

The refrain in the key of Bb may be found in The United Methodist Hymnal, *641.*

WORDS: Richard Blanchard
MUSIC: Richard Blanchard
© 1964 Word Music, LLC

FILL MY CUP
Irr. with Refrain

quench this thirst-ing of my soul; bread of heav-en, feed me 'til I

want no more — fill my cup, fill it up and make me whole!

3094

Come to Me

Come to me, come to me, weak and heav-y lad-en; ___
lad-en, lad-en; ___
lad-en; ___

trust in me, lean on me. I will give you rest. ___

WORDS: Paraphrased from Matthew 11:28
MUSIC: John L. Bell

COME TO ME
66.65

Paraphrase and music © 2008 WGRG, Iona Community (Scotland), admin. by GIA Publications, Inc.

3095 Somebody's Knockin' at Your Door

Refrain
a cappella

Some-bod-y's knock-in' at your door; some-bod-y's

knock-in' at your door; O sin-ner, why don't you

WORDS: African American spiritual
MUSIC: African American spiritual, harm. by Richard Proulx

SOMEBODY'S KNOCKIN'
Irr.

Harm. © 1986 GIA Publications, Inc.

Gentle Shepherd

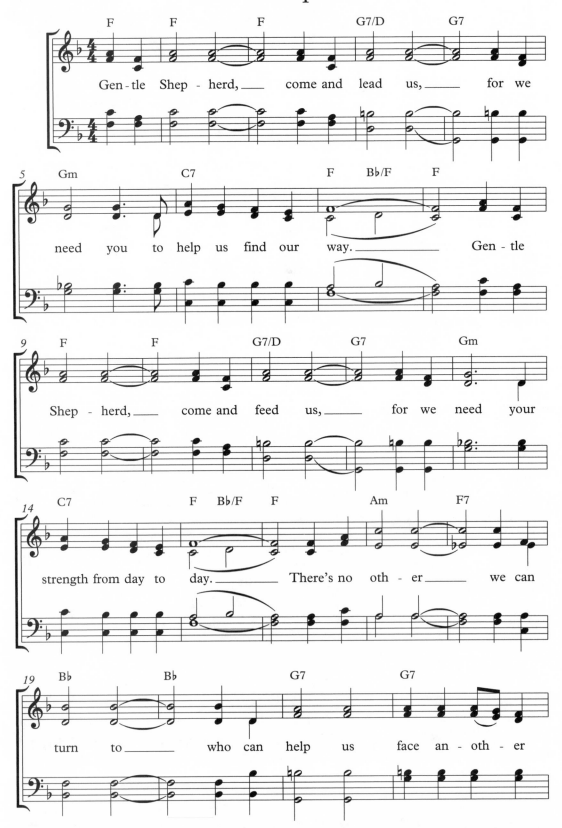

WORDS: Gloria Gaither
MUSIC: William J. Gaither

GENTLE SHEPHERD
Irr.

Depth of Mercy 3097

1. Depth of mer-cy! Can there be mer-cy still re-served for
2. I have long with-stood his grace, long pro-voked him to his
3. I my Mas-ter have de-nied, I a-fresh have cru-ci-
4. There for me the Sav-ior stands, shows his wounds and spreads his
5. Now in-cline me to re-pent, let me now my sins la-

me? Can my God his wrath for-bear, me, the
face, would not heark-en to his calls, grieved him
fied, oft pro-faned his hal-lowed name, put him
hands. God is love! I know, I feel; Je-sus
ment, now my foul re-volt de-plore, weep, be-

chief of sin-ners spare, me, the chief of sin-ners spare?
by a thou-sand falls, grieved him by a thou-sand falls.
to an o-pen shame, put him to an o-pen shame.
weeps and loves me still, Je-sus weeps and loves me still.
lieve, and sin no more, weep, be-lieve, and sin no more.

WORDS: Charles Wesley
MUSIC: Penny Rodriguez

GOTTES ZEIT
77.77

3098

Dust and Ashes

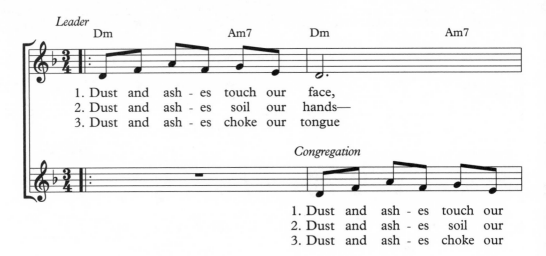

Leader

Dm   Am7   Dm   Am7

1. Dust and ash - es touch our face,
2. Dust and ash - es soil our hands—
3. Dust and ash - es choke our tongue

Congregation

1. Dust and ash - es touch our
2. Dust and ash - es soil our
3. Dust and ash - es choke our

Gm7   Am7   G   Gm7

mark our fail - ure and our fall - ing.   Ho - ly Spir - it, come,
greed of mar - ket, pride of na - tion.   Ho - ly Spir - it, come,
in the waste - land of de - pres - sion.   Ho - ly Spir - it, come,

face,   mark our fail - ure and our fall - ing.
hands—   greed of mar - ket, pride of na - tion.
tongue   in the waste - land of de - pres - sion.

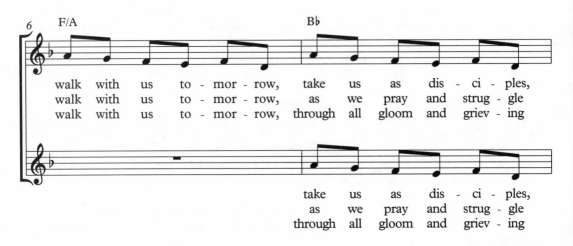

F/A   Bb

walk with us to - mor - row, take us as dis - ci - ples,
walk with us to - mor - row, as we pray and strug - gle
walk with us to - mor - row, through all gloom and griev - ing

take us as dis - ci - ples,
as we pray and strug - gle
through all gloom and griev - ing

WORDS: Brian Wren
MUSIC: David Haas

DUST AND ASHES
7 8.11 14 with Refrain

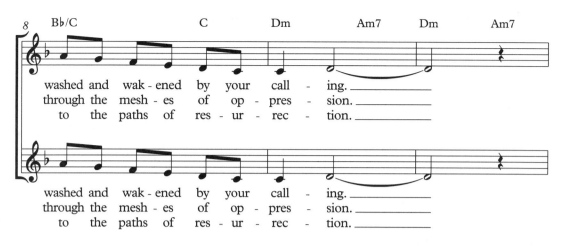

washed and wak-ened by your call - ing. _____
through the mesh - es of op - pres - sion. _____
to the paths of res - ur - rec - tion. _____

washed and wak-ened by your call - ing. _____
through the mesh - es of op - pres - sion. _____
to the paths of res - ur - rec - tion. _____

Refrain

Take us by the hand and lead us, lead us through the des-ert

Take us by the hand and lead us,

sands, bring us liv - ing wa - ter, Ho-ly Spir - it,

lead us through the des-ert sands, bring us liv - ing wa - ter,

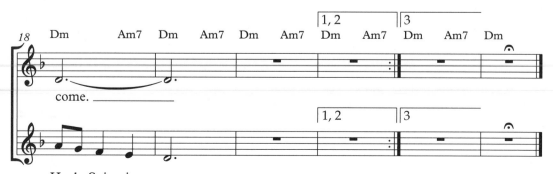

come. _____

Ho-ly Spir - it, come.

3099
Falling on My Knees

WORDS: Kathryn Scott
MUSIC: Kathryn Scott

FALLING ON MY KNEES
67.94 with Refrain

3100 Jesus Paid It All

1. I hear the Sav-ior say, "Thy strength in-deed is small.
2. Lord, now in-deed I find thy power, and thine a-lone
3. For noth-ing good have I where-by thy grace to claim;
4. And when, be-fore the throne, I stand in him com-plete,

Child of weak-ness, watch and pray, find in me thine all in all."
Can change the lep-er's spots and melt the heart of stone.
I'll wash my gar-ments clean in the blood of Cal-vary's Lamb.
"Je-sus died my soul to save," my lips shall still re-peat.

Refrain

Je - sus paid it all, all to him I owe;

sin had left a crim-son stain, he washed it white as snow.

WORDS: Elvina M. Hall
MUSIC: John T. Grape

ALL TO CHRIST
66.77 with Refrain

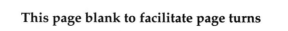
This page blank to facilitate page turns

3101

Love Lifted Me

1. I was sink-ing deep in sin, far from the peace-ful shore,
2. Souls in dan-ger, look a-bove, Je-sus com-plete-ly saves;

ver-y deep-ly stained with-in, sink-ing to rise no more;
he will lift you by his love out of the an-gry waves.

but the Mas-ter of the sea heard my de-spair-ing cry,
He's the Mas-ter of the sea, bil-lows his will o-bey;

from the wa-ters lift-ed me; now safe am I.
he your Sav-ior wants to be — be saved to-day.

WORDS: James Rowe
MUSIC: Howard E. Smith

LOVE LIFTED ME
76.74 with Refrain

You Are My King

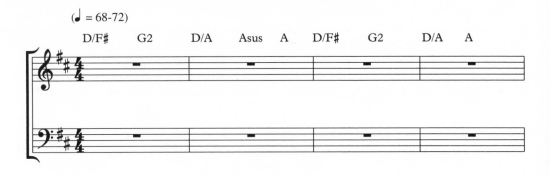

I'm for-giv - en be-cause you were for-sak - en.

I'm ac-cept - ed; you were con-demned.

I'm a-live and well, your Spir-it is with-in me be-

WORDS: Billy James Foote
MUSIC: Billy James Foote

© 1999 worshiptogether.com Songs, admin. at EMICMGPublishing.com

AMAZING LOVE
Irr. with Refrain

_ do I hon-or you. _

Purify My Heart

3103

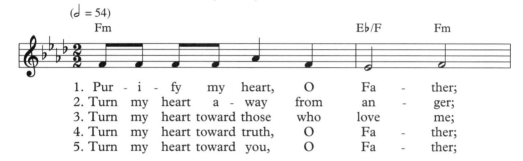

1. Pur - i - fy my heart, O Fa - ther;
2. Turn my heart a - way from an - ger;
3. Turn my heart toward those who love me;
4. Turn my heart toward truth, O Fa - ther;
5. Turn my heart toward you, O Fa - ther;

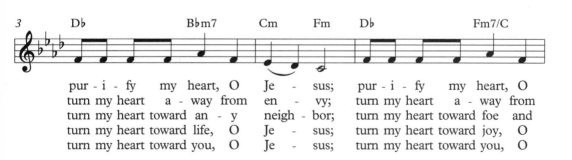

pur - i - fy my heart, O Je - sus; pur - i - fy my heart, O
turn my heart a - way from en - vy; turn my heart a - way from
turn my heart toward an - y neigh - bor; turn my heart toward foe and
turn my heart toward life, O Je - sus; turn my heart toward joy, O
turn my heart toward you, O Je - sus; turn my heart toward you, O

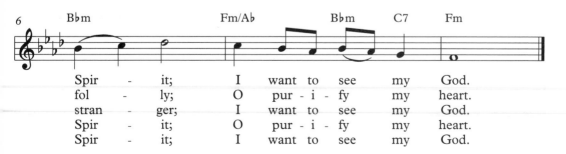

Spir - it; I want to see my God.
fol - ly; O pur - i - fy my heart.
stran - ger; I want to see my God.
Spir - it; O pur - i - fy my heart.
Spir - it; I want to see my God.

WORDS: Richard Leach
MUSIC: Amanda Husberg

TURN MY HEART
88.86

3104

Amazing Grace
(My Chains Are Gone)

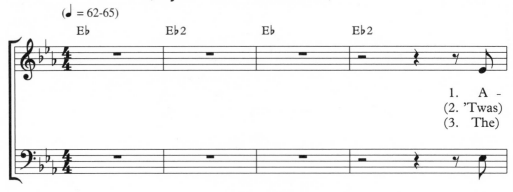

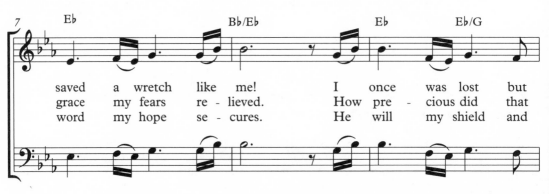

WORDS: John Newton (sts.); refrain by Chris Tomlin and Louie Giglio
MUSIC: Tradional American melody; refrain and arr. by Chris Tomlin and Louis Giglio

MY CHAINS ARE GONE
Irr.

Refrain and arr. © 2006 worshiptogether.com Songs/sixsteps Music (ASCAP), Vamos Publishing (ASCAP), admin. at EMICMGPublishing.com

4. The earth shall soon dis - solve like snow, the sun for - bear to shine. But God who called me here be - low, will be for - ev - er mine, will be for - ev - er mine. You are for - ev - er mine.

In Christ Alone

WORDS: Keith Getty and Stuart Townend
MUSIC: Keith Getty and Stuart Townend

IN CHRIST ALONE
LMD

peace, when fears are stilled, when striv-ings cease! My Com-fort-
died the wrath of God was sat-is-fied; for ev-ery
ry, sin's curse has lost its grip on me. For I am
plan can ev-er pluck me from his hand. 'Til he re-

er, my all in all, here in the love of Christ I
sin on him was laid. Here in the death of Christ I
his and he is mine, bought with the pre-cious blood of
turns or calls me home, here in the power of Christ I'll

stand. 2. In Christ a-
live. 3. There in the
Christ. 4. No guilt in
stand.

Christ. 4. No guilt in life, no fear in death, this is the

3106

Your Grace Is Enough

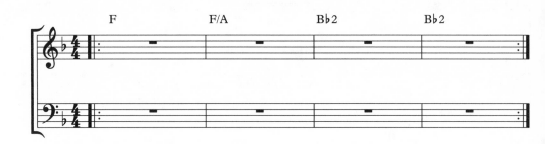

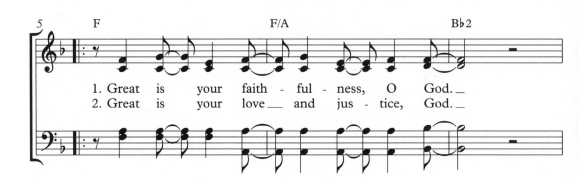

1. Great is your faith - ful - ness, O God. __
2. Great is your love __ and jus - tice, God. __

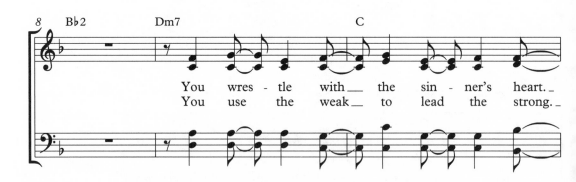

You wres - tle with __ the sin - ner's heart.
You use the weak __ to lead the strong.

You lead us by __ still wa - ters in -
You lead us in __ the song of your __

WORDS: Matt Maher
MUSIC: Matt Maher

YOUR GRACE IS ENOUGH
Irr.

Sing first time only

3107 Just a Little Talk with Jesus

1. I once was lost in sin but Je-sus took me in,
2. Some-times my path seems drear, with-out a ray of cheer,
3. I may have doubts and fears, my eyes be filled with tears,

and then a lit-tle light from heav-en filled my soul;
and then a cloud of doubt may hide the light of day;
but Je-sus is a friend who watch-es day and night;

it bathed my heart in love and wrote my name a-bove,
the mists of sin may rise and hide the star-ry skies,
I go to him in prayer, he knows my ev-ery care,

and just a lit-tle talk with Je-sus made me whole.
but just a lit-tle talk with Je-sus clears the way.
and just a lit-tle talk with Je-sus makes it right.

Refrain

Now let us

WORDS: Cleavant Derricks
MUSIC: Cleavant Derricks

© 1937 Bridge Building (BMI)

JUST A LITTLE TALK
6 6 12 D with Refrain

have a lit-tle talk with Je - sus, tell him all a-bout our trou-bles,
let us he will

hear our faint-est cry, an-swer by and by;
and he will now when you

feel a lit-tle prayer wheel turn-ing, know a lit-tle fire is burn-ing,
and you you will

find a lit-tle talk with Je - sus makes it right, makes it right.
right.

3108

Tradin' My Sorrows

WORDS: Darrell Evans
MUSIC: Darrell Evans

TRADIN' MY SORROWS
Irr.

3109 Living Spirit, Holy Fire

WORDS: Ruth Duck
MUSIC: Lori True
Words © 2005, music © 2007 GIA Publications, Inc.

ALL THINGS NEW
77.77

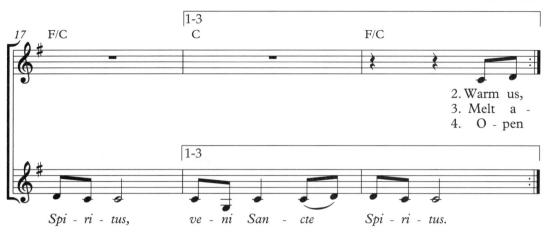

2. Warm us,
3. Melt a -
4. O - pen

Spi - ri - tus, ve - ni San - cte Spi - ri - tus.

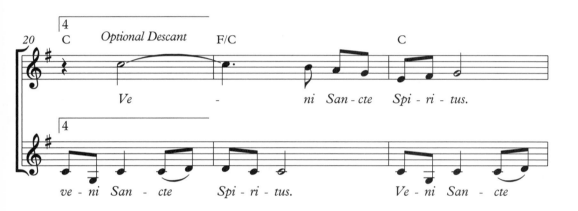

Optional Descant

Ve - ni San - cte Spi - ri - tus.

ve - ni San - cte Spi - ri - tus. Ve - ni San - cte

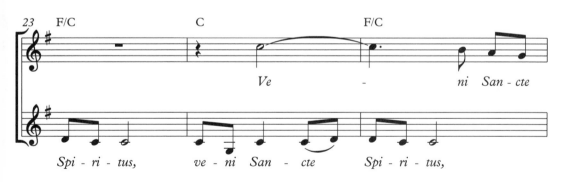

Ve - ni San - cte

Spi - ri - tus, ve - ni San - cte Spi - ri - tus,

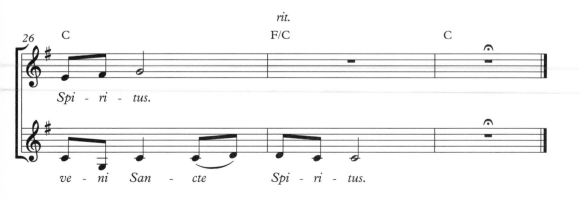

rit.

Spi - ri - tus.

ve - ni San - cte Spi - ri - tus.

3110 By Grace We Have Been Saved

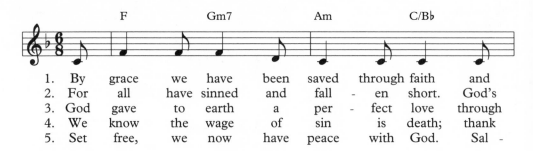

1. By grace we have been saved through faith and
2. For all have sinned and fall - en short. God's
3. God gave to earth a per - fect love through
4. We know the wage of sin is death; thank
5. Set free, we now have peace with God. Sal -

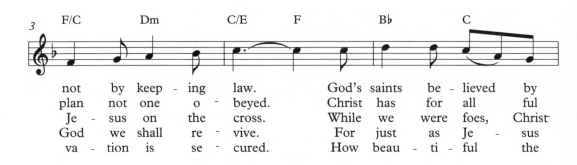

not by keep - ing law. God's saints be - lieved by
plan not one o - beyed. Christ has for all ful
Je - sus on the cross. While we were foes, Christ
God we shall re - vive. For just as Je - sus
va - tion is se - cured. How beau - ti - ful the

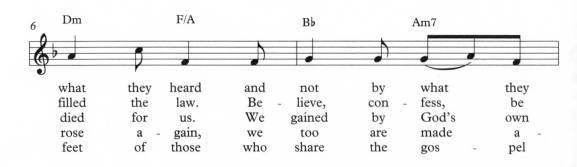

what they heard and not by what they
filled the law. Be - lieve, con - fess, be
died for us. We gained by God's own
rose a - gain, we too are made a -
feet of those who share the gos - pel

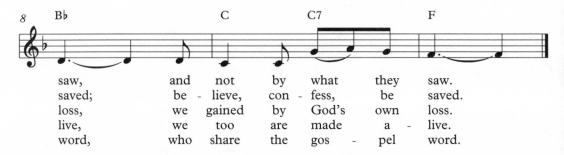

saw, and not by what they saw.
saved; be - lieve, con - fess, be saved.
loss, we gained by God's own loss.
live, we too are made a - live.
word, who share the gos - pel word.

WORDS: Rusty Edwards   DOVE OF PEACE
MUSIC: *The Southern Harmony;* harm. by Charles H. Webb   CM

Redemption

The choral parts may be sung softly underneath the Leader parts.
**Optional harmony on stanzas 2 and 3.*

WORDS: Josh Tinley
MUSIC: Josh Tinley
© 2008 Josh Tinley

REDEMPTION
Irr. with Refrain

3112

Breathe

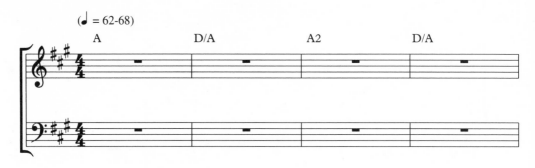

First time: Unison
Second time: Parts

This is the air____ I breathe, this is the air____

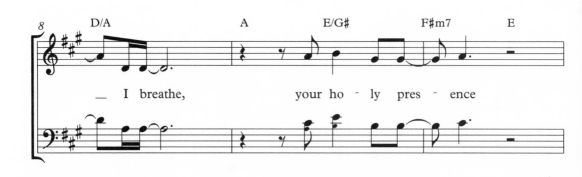

____ I breathe, your ho - ly pres - ence

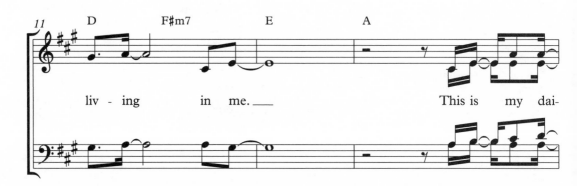

liv - ing in me.____ This is my dai-

WORDS: Marie Barnett
MUSIC: Marie Barnett

BREATHE
Irr. with Refrain

ly bread, this is my dai - ly bread,

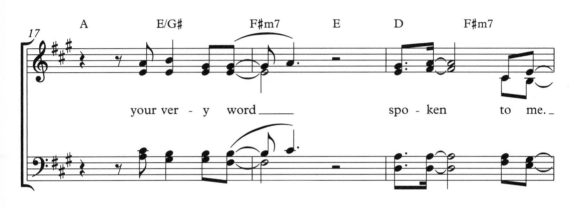

your ver - y word _____ spo - ken to me. _

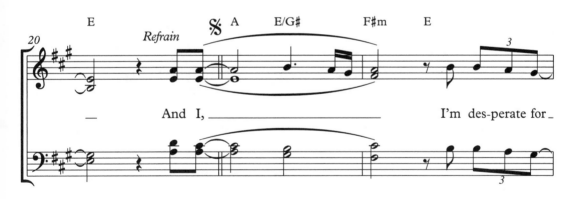

_ And I, _____ I'm des-perate for _

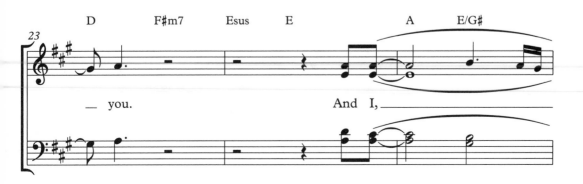

_ you. And I, _____

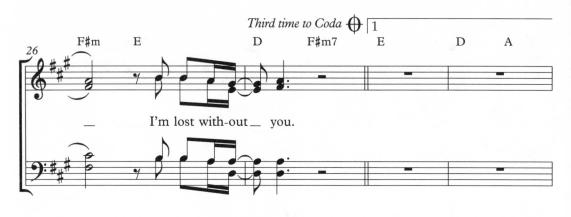

Third time to Coda

I'm lost with-out__ you.

This is the air__ And I,__

CODA

This is the air__ I breathe,

this is the air__ I breathe.

A Wilderness Wandering People

3113

WORDS: Jim Strathdee
MUSIC: Jim Strathdee
© 1996 Desert Flower Music

WILDERNESS
Irr.

3114 Come to the Water

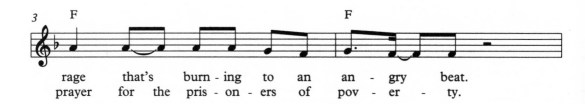

1. There's a war go-ing on just a-cross the street, there's a
(2. There's a) cry from the child in the fac-to-ry, there's a

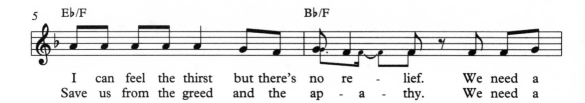

rage that's burn-ing to an an-gry beat.
prayer for the pris-on-ers of pov-er-ty.

I can feel the thirst but there's no re-lief. We need a
Save us from the greed and the ap-a-thy. We need a

riv-er. There's a sound in the dis-tance like a
riv-er. There's a hope like a flood run-ning

thun-der cloud, we're wait-ing for the rain while the
down our street, we're an ar-my of peace-mak-ers

sun beats down. Can you feel it ris-ing from the
on our feet. Take us to the place love and

WORDS: Paul Baloche, Steven Curtis-Chapman, Stuart Garrard, Israel Houghton,
Tim Hughes, Graham Kendrick, Andy Park, Matt Redman, Martin Smith,
Michael W. Smith, Chris Tomlin, and Darlene Zschech
MUSIC: Paul Baloche, Steven Curtis-Chapman, Stuart Garrard, Israel Houghton,
Tim Hughes, Graham Kendrick, Andy Park, Matt Redman, Martin Smith,
Michael W. Smith, Chris Tomlin, and Darlene Zschech

COME TO THE WATER
Irr.

Come to the water

14 Bb/F   F   F

un - der - ground? We need a riv - er.
mer - cy meet. There is a riv - er.

17 A/C#   A/C#   Dm

Oh, let jus - tice roll like riv - ers.

20 Dm   A/C#   A/C#   Dm

Oh, let mer - cy flow with love, __ love. __

Third time to Coda ⊕ *Refrain*

24 Eb   F   F   Cm7

__ Come to the wa - ter, come to the wa-

28 Cm7   Bb   Bb

ter of life. __ It will nev - er run dry.

31 F   F   Cm7

Come to the wa - ter, run to the wa-

34 Cm7   Bb   Bb

ter of life. __ It will nev - er run dry.

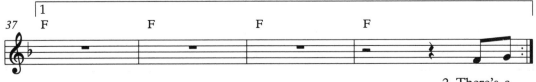

1

37 F   F   F   F

2. There's a

Covenant Prayer

3115

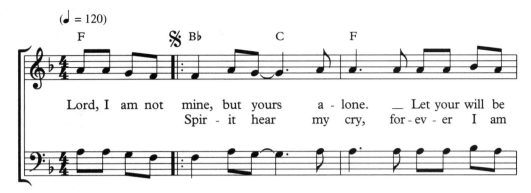

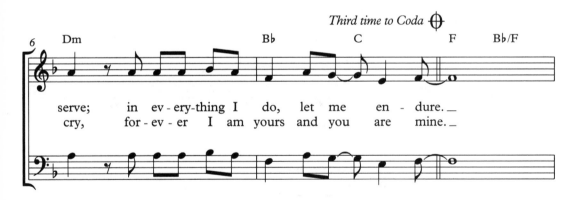

WORDS: John Wesley
MUSIC: Jay D. Locklear and Adam Seate

Music © 2008 Jay D. Locklear and Adam Seate

COVENANT
Irr.

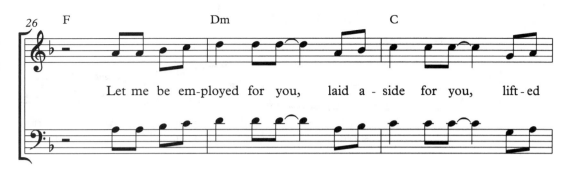

Let me be em-ployed for you, laid a - side for you, lift - ed high for you or brought low.

Let me be full, let me be emp-ty.

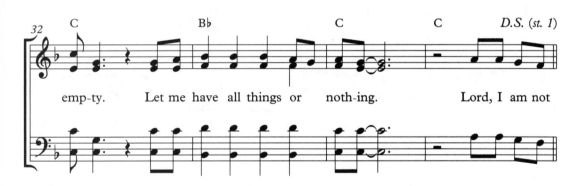

Let me have all things or noth-ing. Lord, I am not

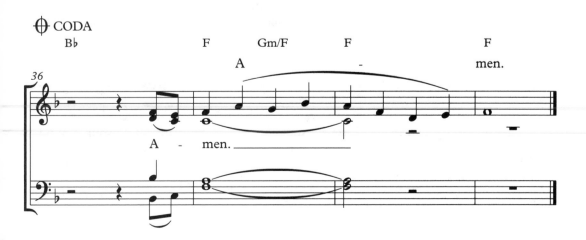

CODA

A - men. A - men.

3116

Love the Lord

WORDS: Lincoln Brewster
MUSIC: Lincoln Brewster

LOVE THE LORD
Irr.

3117 Rule of Life

Moderately slow (♩ = 88)

Do all the good you can, _____ by all the means you can, _____

_ in all the ways you can, _____ in all the plac-es you can, _____

_ at all the times you can, _____ to all the peo-ple you can, _____

_ as long as ev - er _____ you can. _____

WORDS: 18th cent. aphorism, attr. to John Wesley
MUSIC: Edward Bonnemere, arr. by Cynthia Wilson

RULE OF LIFE
Irr.

3118 Take This Moment, Sign, and Space

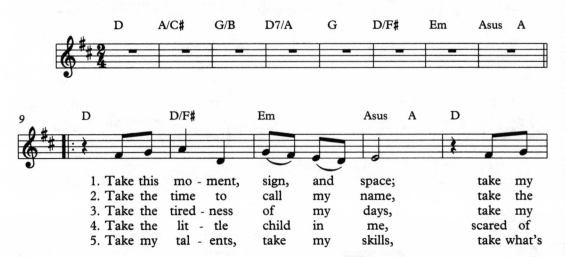

1. Take this mo - ment, sign, and space; take my
2. Take the time to call my name, take the
3. Take the tired - ness of my days, take my
4. Take the lit - tle child in me, scared of
5. Take my tal - ents, take my skills, take what's

WORDS: John L. Bell
MUSIC: John L. Bell and Graham Maule

TAKE THIS MOMENT
75.75

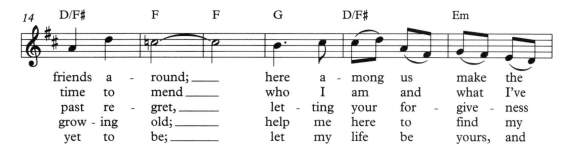

friends a - round;____ here a - mong us make the
time to mend____ who I am and what I've
past re - gret,____ let - ting your for - give - ness
grow - ing old;____ help me here to find my
yet to be;____ let my life be yours, and

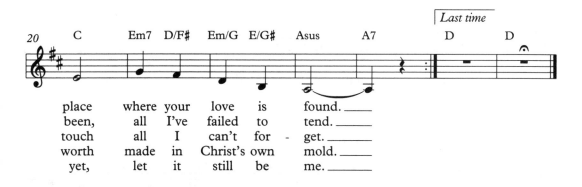

place where your love is found.____
been, all I've failed to tend.____
touch all I can't for - get.____
worth made in Christ's own mold.____
yet, let it still be me.____

Take, O Take Me As I Am 3119

Gently (♩ = ca. 84)

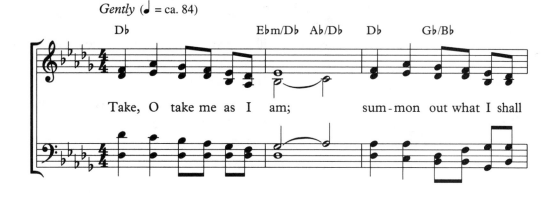

Take, O take me as I am; sum - mon out what I shall

be; set your seal up - on my heart and live in me.

WORDS: John L. Bell
MUSIC: John L. Bell

TAKE, O TAKE
7 7 11

3120   Amazing Abundance

1. A - maz - ing a -

bun - dance poured out on this land, ___ the mark of your

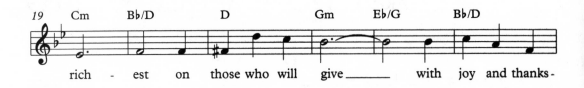

gra - cious and gen - er - ous hand. ___ Your bless - ing is

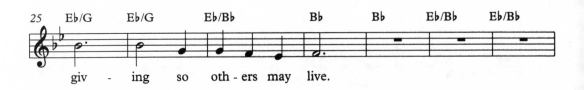

rich - est on those who will give ___ with joy and thanks-

giv - ing so oth - ers may live.

2. A   ho - ly com - pas - sion is born through the
(3. We) pray for com - mun - ion, all na - tions so

WORDS: Laurie Zelman
MUSIC: Mark A. Miller

ABUNDANCE
65.65 D with Refrain

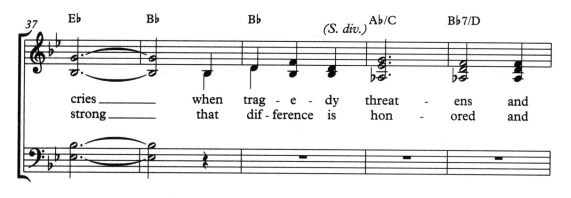

cries _____ when trag - e - dy threat - ens and
strong _____ that dif - ference is hon - ored and

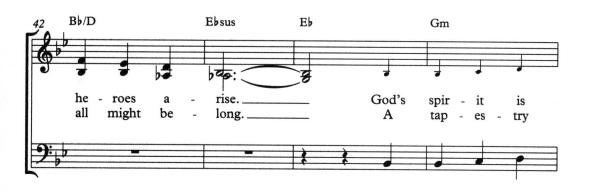

he - roes a - rise. _____ God's spir - it is
all might be - long. _____ A tap - es - try

pres - ent and felt ev - ery - where _____ that
wov - en by myr - i - ad hands, _____ a

hands reach through dark - ness and bat - tle des -
ban - ner of free - dom the bright braid - ed

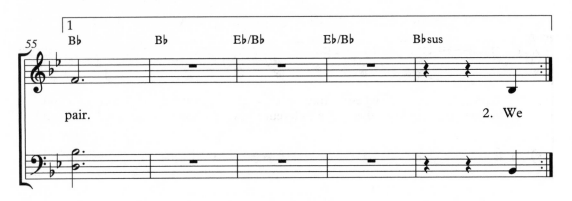

pair.   2. We

strands.   Praise God for the na - tions, O help us to

see _____   the whole world is yours, Lord, and

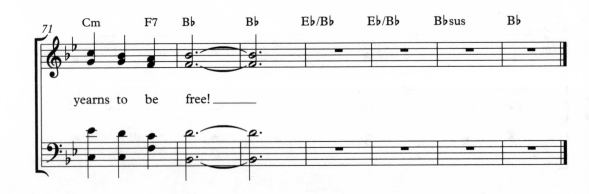

yearns to be free! _____

If You Believe and I Believe

Moderato
a cappella

If you be-lieve and I be-lieve and we to-geth-er pray,

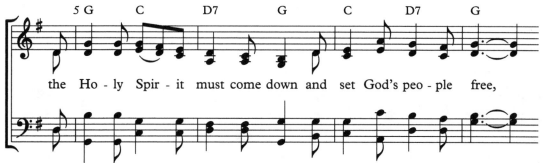

the Ho-ly Spir-it must come down and set God's peo-ple free,

and set God's peo-ple free, and set God's peo-ple free;

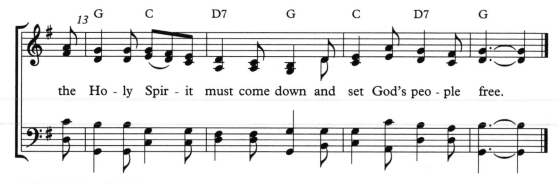

the Ho-ly Spir-it must come down and set God's peo-ple free.

WORDS: Traditional Zimbabwe
MUSIC: Traditional Zimbabwe; arr. by John L. Bell

IF YOU BELIEVE
Irr.

3122   Christ Has Broken Down the Wall

1. Christ has bro-ken down the wall,
2. We're ac-cept-ed as we are,
3. Cast a-side your doubts and fears,
4. We will tear down the walls!

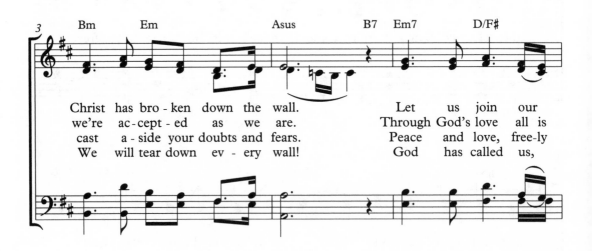

Christ has bro-ken down the wall. Let us join our
we're ac-cept-ed as we are. Through God's love all is
cast a-side your doubts and fears. Peace and love, free-ly
We will tear down ev-ery wall! God has called us,

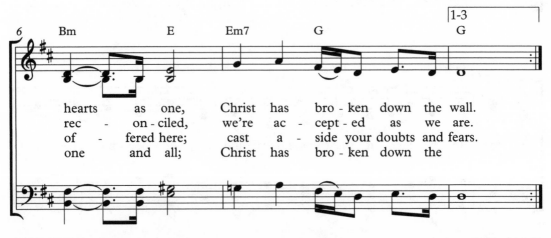

hearts as one, Christ has bro-ken down the wall.
rec - on-ciled, we're ac - cept-ed as we are.
of - fered here; cast a - side your doubts and fears.
one and all; Christ has bro-ken down the

WORDS: Mark A. Miller
MUSIC: Mark A. Miller
© 2011 Choristers Guild

BROKEN WALLS
Irr.

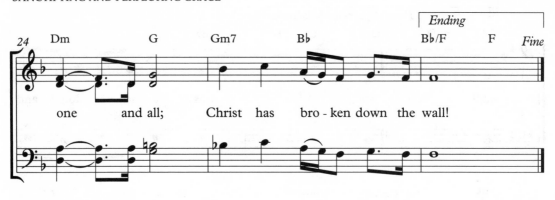

one and all; Christ has bro-ken down the wall!

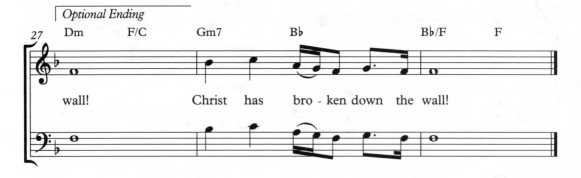

Optional Ending

wall! Christ has bro-ken down the wall!

3123   Here Is Peace

1. Here is peace, when grace a-stounds us quell-ing
2. Here is peace, when grace en-gen-ders love that
3. Here is peace, when grace sur-pris-es ig-no-

all our wild pre-tense. Here is peace, sha-lom and
nei-ther fades nor ends. Here is peace when peo-ple
rance with words of hope. Here is peace to light our

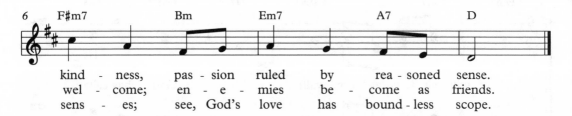

kind-ness, pas-sion ruled by rea-soned sense.
wel-come; en-e-mies be-come as friends.
sens-es; see, God's love has bound-less scope.

WORDS: Andrew Pratt   HERE IS PEACE
MUSIC: Traditional Latvian melody   87.87

How Shall I Come Before the Lord 3124

1. How shall I come be-fore the Lord and bow my-
2. Will fin-est gifts bring God's de-light? Will wealth bring
3. Let jus-tice shine in all your ways. Let lov-ing

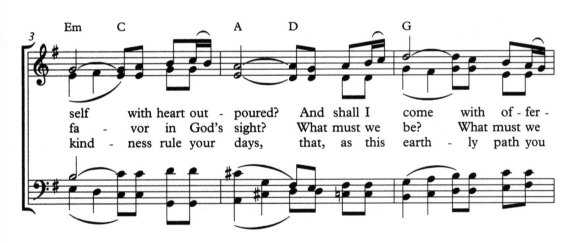

self with heart out-poured? And shall I come with of-fer-
fa-vor in God's sight? What must we be? What must we
kind-ness rule your days, that, as this earth-ly path you

ing? What shall I give? What shall I bring?
do? What does the Lord re-quire of you?
trod, you shall walk hum-bly with your God.

WORDS: Dean McIntyre
MUSIC: English folk melody; harm. by Dean McIntyre

O WALY WALY
LM

3125 Peace for the Children

1. Peace for the chil - dren, peace, peace.
2. Peace for the wom - en, peace, peace.
3. Peace for the men, peace, peace.
4. Peace in our fam - i - lies, peace, peace.
5. Peace for the na - tions, peace, peace.

Peace for the chil-dren we pray. Fol-low-ing the path of
Peace for the wom-en we pray. Fol-low-ing the path of
Peace for the men we pray. Fol-low-ing the path of
Peace in our fam-ilies we pray. Fol-low-ing the path of
Peace for the na-tions we pray. Fol-low-ing the path of

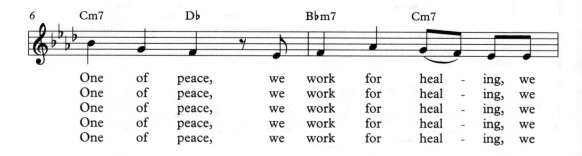

One of peace, we work for heal - ing, we
One of peace, we work for heal - ing, we
One of peace, we work for heal - ing, we
One of peace, we work for heal - ing, we
One of peace, we work for heal - ing, we

work for peace; peace for the chil-dren to - day.
work for peace; peace for the wom-en to - day.
work for peace; peace for the men to - day.
work for peace; peace for our fam-ilies to - day.
work for peace; peace for the na-tions to - day.

6. Peace for the creatures...
7. Peace for our planet...
8. Peace in the universe...

9. *Hum this verse softly, during which time individuals may call out the word "peace" in other languages, making a global connection.*

10. Peace in the soul...

WORDS: Doreen Lankshear-Smith
MUSIC: Doreen Lankshear-Smith

PEACE FOR ALL
Irr.

TRANSPOSE - 3

Everything That Has Voice

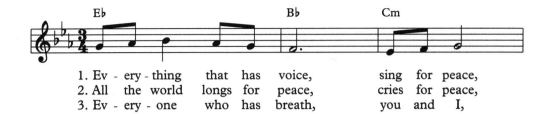

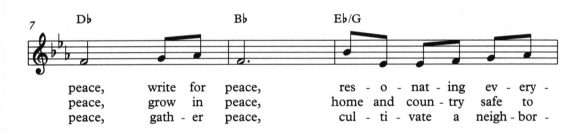

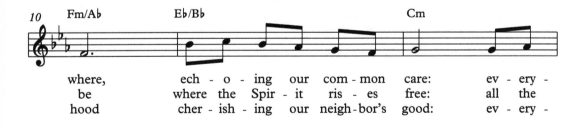

1. Ev-ery-thing that has voice, sing for peace,
2. All the world longs for peace, cries for peace,
3. Ev-ery-one who has breath, you and I,

speak for peace, giv-en chance, giv-en choice, work for
dies for peace; let the chil-dren, ev-ery place, sleep in
pass-ers-by, ev-ery ten-ant of the earth, plant for

peace, write for peace, res-o-nat-ing ev-ery-
peace, grow in peace, home and coun-try safe to
peace, gath-er peace, cul-ti-vate a neigh-bor-

where, ech-o-ing our com-mon care: ev-ery-
be where the Spir-it ris-es free: all the
hood cher-ish-ing our neigh-bor's good: ev-ery-

thing that has voice sing for peace!
world longs for peace cries for peace.
one who has breath live in peace.

WORDS: Shirley Erena Murray
MUSIC: Marty Haugen

SING FOR PEACE
66.76.779

3127 I Have a Dream

1. "I have a dream," a man once said, "where
2. But in this world of bit - ter strife the
3. Fierce per - se - cu - tion, war, and hate are
4. So dream the dreams and sing the songs, but
5. Lord, give us vi - sion, make us strong, help

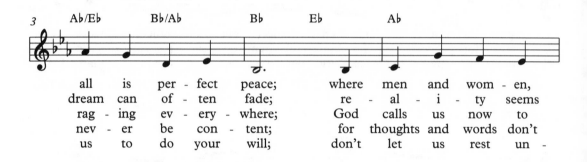

all is per - fect peace; where men and wom - en,
dream can of - ten fade; re - al - i - ty seems
rag - ing ev - ery - where; God calls us now to
nev - er be con - tent; for thoughts and words don't
us to do your will; don't let us rest un -

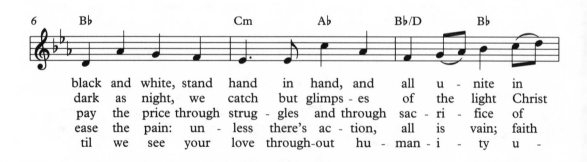

black and white, stand hand in hand, and all u - nite in
dark as night, we catch but glimps - es of the light Christ
pay the price through strug - gles and through sac - ri - fice of
ease the pain: un - less there's ac - tion, all is vain; faith
til we see your love through-out hu - man - i - ty u -

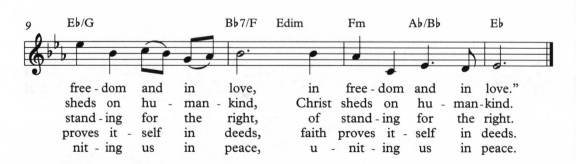

free - dom and in love, in free - dom and in love."
sheds on hu - man - kind, Christ sheds on hu - man - kind.
stand - ing for the right, of stand - ing for the right.
proves it - self in deeds, faith proves it - self in deeds.
nit - ing us in peace, u - nit - ing us in peace.

WORDS: Pamela J. Pettitt
MUSIC: Charles Hubert Hastings Parry

REPTON
86.886

Words © Pam Pettitt

3128   5 vs.   Whatever You Do

USE: PGS. 1-3 IN FESTIVAL HYMNS w/ DESCANTS BY MARIE POOLER

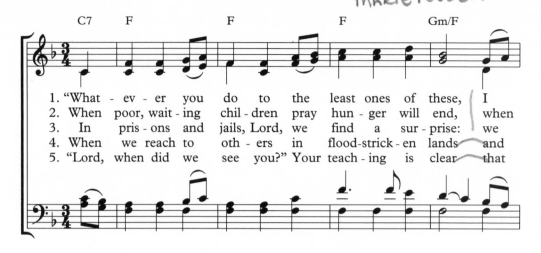

1. "What-ev-er you do to the least ones of these, I
2. When poor, wait-ing chil-dren pray hun-ger will end, when
3. In pris-ons and jails, Lord, we find a sur-prise: we
4. When we reach to oth-ers in flood-strick-en lands and
5. "Lord, when did we see you?" Your teach-ing is clear that

tell you in truth that you do un-to me!" Lord
those long-for-got-ten cry out for a friend, when
see you in peo-ple whom oth-ers de-spise. At
of-fer our hearts there, and of-fer our hands, we
when we serve oth-ers, we're serv-ing you here. And

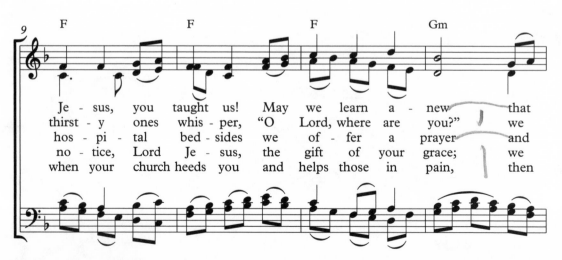

Je-sus, you taught us! May we learn a-new that
thirst-y ones whis-per, "O Lord, where are you?" we
hos-pi-tal bed-sides we of-fer a prayer and
no-tice, Lord Je-sus, the gift of your grace; we
when your church heeds you and helps those in pain, then

WORDS: Carolyn Winfrey Gillette
MUSIC: William J. Kirkpatrick; arr. by David Willcocks

CRADLE SONG
11 11.11 11

Words © 2008 Carolyn Winfrey Gillette; arr. © 1960 Oxford University Press

when we serve oth - ers, we al - so serve you.
hear, in their long - ing, that you're call - ing, too.
find, when we vis - it the sick, you are there.
see, in the crowds of the suf - fering, your face.
out of the cha - os, hope ris - es a - gain.

Touch the Earth Lightly

3129

(♩ = 100)

1. Touch the earth light - ly, use the earth gent - ly,
2. We who en - dan - ger, who cre - ate hun - ger,
3. Let there be green - ing, birth from the burn - ing,
4. God of all liv - ing, God of all lov - ing,

nour - ish the life of the world in our care:
a - gents of death for all crea - tures that live,
wa - ter that bless - es and air that is sweet,
God of the seed - ling, the snow, and the sun,

gift of great won - der, ours to sur - ren - der,
we who would fos - ter clouds of dis - as - ter,
health in God's gar - den, hope in God's chil - dren,
teach us, de - flect us, Christ, re - con - nect us,

trust for the chil - dren to - mor - row will bear.
God of our plan - et, fore - stall and for - give!
re - gen - er - a - tion that peace will com - plete.
us - ing us gen - tly and mak - ing us one.

WORDS: Shirley Erena Murray
MUSIC: Swee-Hong Lim

AI HU
10 10.10 10

3130
Come, Emmanuel

1., 4. Come and speak to us, come and re-new us, come and live
2. Once mer-cy found us, still you a-stound us, hold and sur-
3. Love that be-gins us, par-dons and wins us, come and reign

through us, Em-man-u - el._____ Grace to im - plore us,
round us, Em-man-u - el._____ Liv - ing in - side us,
in us, Em-man-u - el._____ Come and speak to us,

Last time to Coda

ev - er be - fore us, come and re - store us, Em-man-u - el._____
faith-ful to guide us, cov - er and hide us, Em-man-u - el._____
fill and re - new us, come and live through us, Em-man-u -

Refrain

Come,_____ Em-man-u - el;_____ come,_____ Em-man-u-

el._____ Come,_____ Em-man-u - el;_____ come,_____

Em-man-u - el._____

CODA

el,_____ Em-man-u - el, Em-man-u - el._____

WORDS: Twila Paris
MUSIC: Twila Paris

COME EMMANUEL
10 9.10 9 with Refrain

Hear My Prayer, O God

3131

WORDS: Carl P. Daw, Jr., based on Psalm 143
MUSIC: Hal H. Hopson
Words © 2005, music © 2006 Hope Publishing Company

HYMN CHANT
56.56 D

3132 House of God

WORDS: Mariénne Kreitlow
MUSIC: Mariénne Kreitlow

© 2000 Mariénne Kreitlow, Living Song

HOUSE OF GOD
67.66.88.83

Kyrie

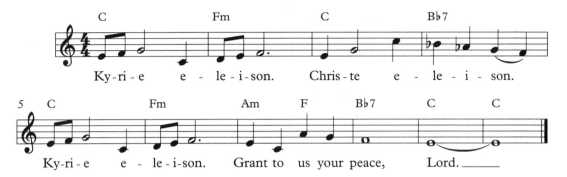

Ky-ri-e   e-le-i-son.   Chris-te   e-le-i-son.

Ky-ri-e   e-le-i-son.   Grant to   us your peace,   Lord._____

MUSIC: Steve Garnaas-Holmes
Music © 1990 Steve Garnaas-Holmes

HAVE MERCY
76.76

Still

3134

1. _ Hide   me   now_   un-der   your   wings._
(2. Find) rest,   my   soul,_   in Christ   a-   lone._

Cov-er   me____   with-in your might-y   hand._   When the o-ceans
Know his   power_   in qui-et-ness   and trust._

rise and thun-ders roar,_   I will soar with You   a-bove   the storm;_

_ Fa-ther, you are king o-ver   the flood._   I will be still_

_ and know you   are God._   2. Find   _ and know you   are God._

WORDS: Reuben Morgan
MUSIC: Reuben Morgan

STILL
Irr. with Refrain

© 2002, arr. © 2010 Reuben Morgan and Hillsong Publishing, admin. in the U.S. and Canada by Integrity Worship Music (ASCAP)
c/o Integrity Media, Inc.

3135 In God Alone

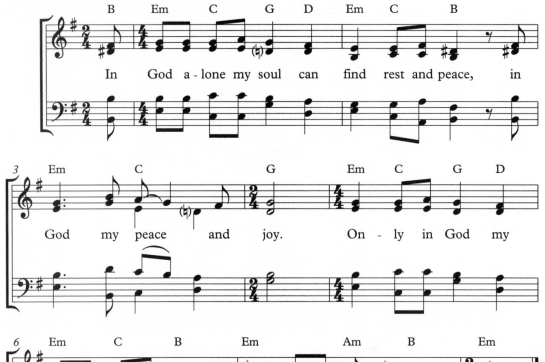

In God a-lone my soul can find rest and peace, in

God my peace and joy. On-ly in God my

soul can find its rest, find its rest and peace.

WORDS: Based on Psalm 62:1
MUSIC: Jacques Berthier

IN GOD ALONE
11 6.10 5

© 1991 Les Presses de Taizé (France), admin. by GIA Publications, Inc.

3136 In the Quiet of This Moment

In the qui-et_____ of this mo-ment_____ there is

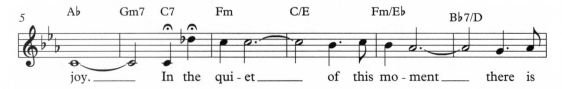

joy._____ In the qui-et_____ of this mo-ment_____ there is

WORDS: Dean McIntyre
MUSIC: Dean McIntyre

QUIET MOMENT
11 11.7 7 11

© 2005 The General Board of Discipleship of The United Methodist Church

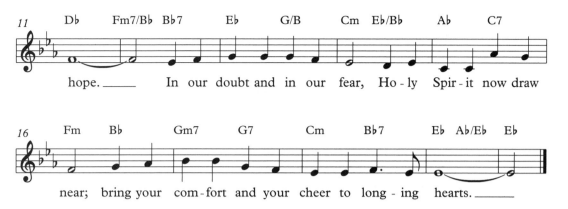

Lord Jesus Christ, Your Light Shines 3137
(Jésus le Christ)

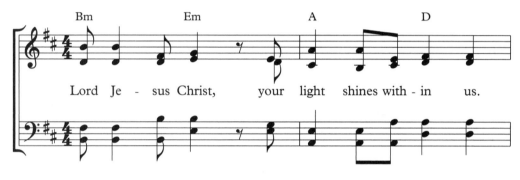

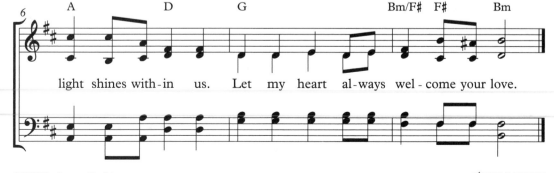

WORDS: Jacques Berthier
MUSIC: Jacques Berthier

JÉSUS LE CHRIST
10 11.10 9

3138

Confession

On repeat only

Soloist/Choir
(Sing upper harmony notes only on stanza 2.)

Congregation

For words we've said _
For ho - ly wars, _

We hum-bly ask the mer - cy of your love. ____

_ and have - n't said. _
_ op - pres - sive mis-sions.

We hum - bly ask the mer - cy of your love. _

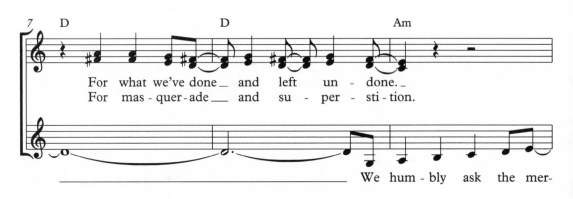

For what we've done _ and left un - done. _
For mas - quer-ade _ and su - per - sti - tion.

We hum - bly ask the mer -

For harm we've planned _ and scars we've left. _
For tak - ing sides _ and lay - ing blame. _

cy of your love. ____ We

WORDS: j. Snodgrass
MUSIC: Isaac Everett

© 2007 j. Snodgrass and Isaac Everett

CONFESSION
Irr.

3139 We Cannot Measure How You Heal

1. We can - not meas - ure how you heal or
2. The pain that will not go a - way, the
3. So some have come who need your help and

an - swer ev - ery suf - ferer's prayer, yet we be -
guilt that clings from things long past, the fear of
some have come to make a - mends, as hands which

lieve your grace re - sponds where faith and doubt u -
what the fu - ture holds are pres - ent as if
shaped and saved the world are pres - ent in the

nite to care. Your hands, though blood - ied on the cross, sur -
meant to last. But pres - ent, too, is love which tends the
touch of friends. Lord, let your Spir - it meet us here to

vive to hold and heal and warn, to car - ry all through
hurt we nev - er hope to find, the pri - vate ag - o -
mend the bod - y, mind and soul, to dis - en - tan - gle

death to life and cra - dle chil - dren yet un - born.
nies in - side, the mem - o - ries that haunt the mind.
peace from pain and make your bro - ken peo - ple whole.

WORDS: John L. Bell
MUSIC: Traditional Scottish melody; harm. by Carlton R. Young

CANDLER
LMD

Give Me Jesus

1. In the morn-ing when I rise, in the morn-ing when I rise, in the morn-ing when I rise, give me Je - sus.
2. I heard my moth-er say, I heard my moth-er say, I heard my moth-er say, give me Je - sus.
3. Dark mid-night was my cry, dark mid-night was my cry, dark mid-night was my cry, give me Je - sus.
4. Oh, when I come to die, oh, when I come to die, oh, when I come to die, give me Je - sus.

Refrain

Give me Je - sus, give me Je - sus, you may have all this world, give me Je - sus.

WORDS: African American spiritual
MUSIC: African American spiritual, harm. by Verolga Nix

GIVE ME JESUS
66.64 with Refrain

3141

Holy Darkness

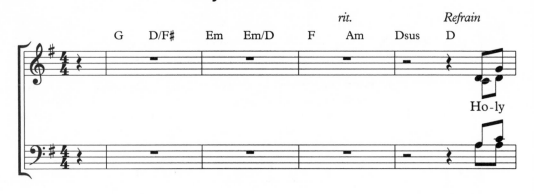

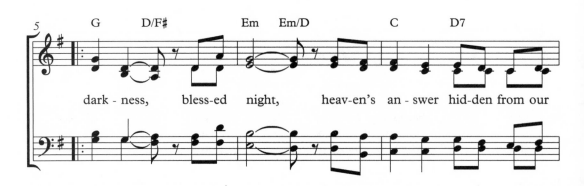

dark - ness, bless-ed night, heav-en's an - swer hid-den from our

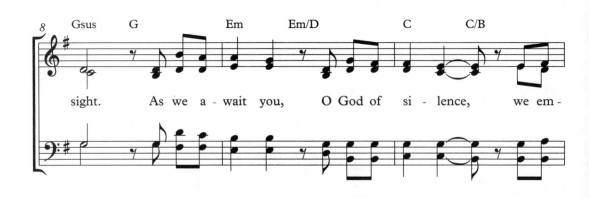

sight. As we a - wait you, O God of si - lence, we em-

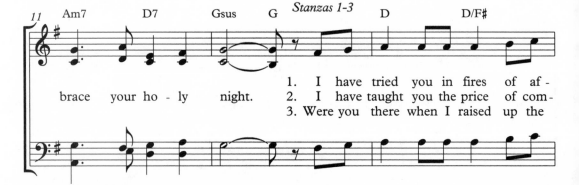

brace your ho - ly night.

Stanzas 1-3

1. I have tried you in fires of af -
2. I have taught you the price of com -
3. Were you there when I raised up the

WORDS: Inspired by St. John of the Cross
MUSIC: Dan Schutte
© 1988, 1993 Daniel L. Schutte

HOLY DARKNESS
Irr. with Refrain

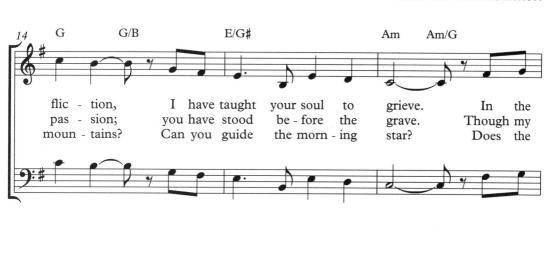

14

G   G/B   E/G#   Am   Am/G

flic - tion,   I have taught your soul to grieve.   In the
pas - sion;   you have stood be - fore the grave.   Though my
moun - tains?   Can you guide the morn - ing star?   Does the

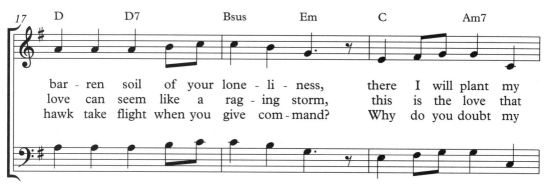

17

D   D7   Bsus   Em   C   Am7

bar - ren soil of your lone - li - ness,   there I will plant my
love can seem like a rag - ing storm,   this is the love that
hawk take flight when you give com - mand?   Why do you doubt my

1, 2   3

20

Dsus   D   Dsus   D   B7/F#   B7

seed.   Ho - ly   power?   4. In your deep - est hour of
saves.   (5. As the) watch - man waits for

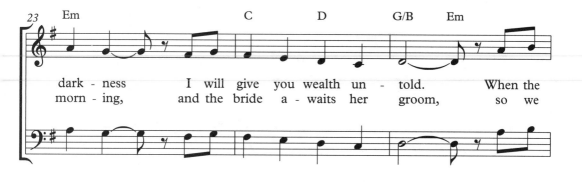

23

Em   C   D   G/B   Em

dark - ness   I will give you wealth un - told.   When the
morn - ing,   and the bride a - waits her groom,   so we

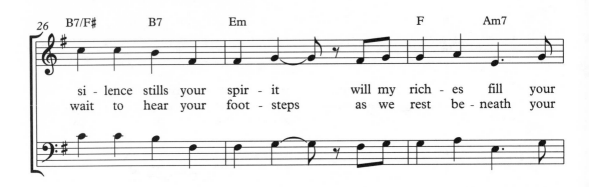

si - lence stills your spir - it   will my rich - es fill your
wait to hear your foot - steps   as we rest be - neath your

soul?
moon.   Ho - ly dark - ness, bless-ed night, heav-en's

an - swer hid-den from our sight   As we a - wait you, O God of

si - lence, we em-brace your ho - ly night. 5. As the night.

I Love the Lord

3142

1. I love the Lord; _____ he heard my cry _____
2. I love the Lord; _____ he heard my cry _____

_____ and pit - ied ev - ery groan. _____ Long as I
_____ and chased my grief a - way. _____ O let my

live _____ and trou - bles rise, _____ I'll has - ten
heart _____ no more des - pair _____ while I have

to _____ his throne.
breath _____ to pray.

WORDS: Psalm 116:1-2; vers. Isaac Watts
MUSIC: African American spiritual; arr. by Richard Smallwood

I LOVE THE LORD
CM

3143   Jesus, You Are the New Day

Refrain
(♩ = 90)

Je - sus,   you are the new day dawn-ing be-fore our   eyes;

Je - sus,   you are the light that   bids   us   rise.

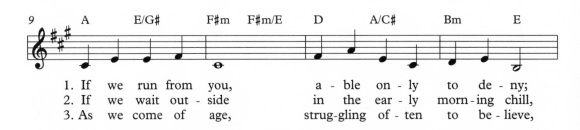

1. If   we   run from   you,   a - ble on - ly   to   de - ny;
2. If   we   wait out - side   in the ear - ly   morn - ing chill,
3. As   we   come of   age,   strug-gling of - ten   to   be - lieve,

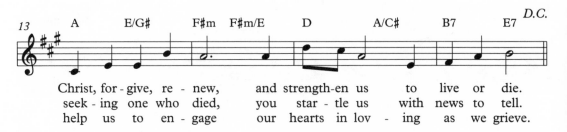

Christ, for - give, re - new,   and strength-en us   to   live   or   die.
seek - ing one who   died,   you   star - tle us   with news to   tell.
help   us   to   en - gage   our   hearts in lov - ing   as   we grieve.

WORDS: Daniel Charles Damon (Luke 24:1-12)   STONYFORD
MUSIC: Daniel Charles Damon   57.58 with Refrain

When the Waves Are Crashing 3144

WORDS: Gareth Hill
MUSIC: Jackson Henry

BLUE MOOD
66.63 D

Words © 2007 Hope Publishing Company; music © 2011 Jackson Henry

3145 Breath of God, Breath of Peace

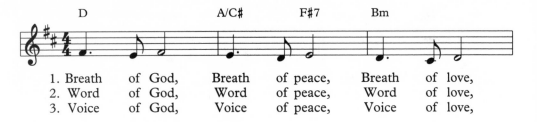

1. Breath of God, Breath of peace, Breath of love,
2. Word of God, Word of peace, Word of love,
3. Voice of God, Voice of peace, Voice of love,

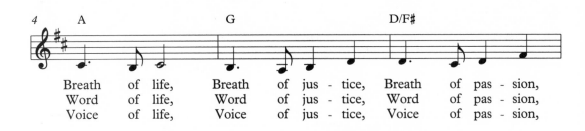

Breath of life, Breath of jus - tice, Breath of pas - sion,
Word of life, Word of jus - tice, Word of pas - sion,
Voice of life, Voice of jus - tice, Voice of pas - sion,

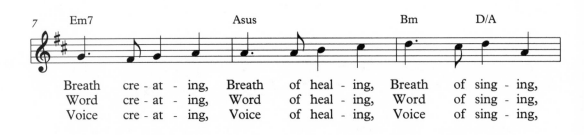

Breath cre - at - ing, Breath of heal - ing, Breath of sing - ing,
Word cre - at - ing, Word of heal - ing, Word of sing - ing,
Voice cre - at - ing, Voice of heal - ing, Voice of sing - ing,

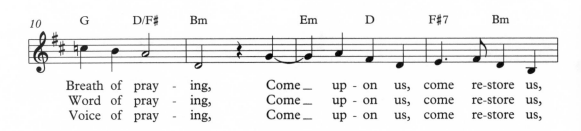

Breath of pray - ing, Come _ up - on us, come re-store us,
Word of pray - ing, Come _ up - on us, come re-store us,
Voice of pray - ing, Come _ up - on us, come re-store us,

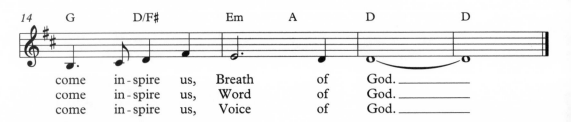

come in - spire us, Breath of God. _____
come in - spire us, Word of God. _____
come in - spire us, Voice of God. _____

WORDS: Adam M. L. Tice
MUSIC: Sally Ann Morris

© 2009 GIA Publications, Inc.

PATTERNS
66.88.887

O Breath of Life

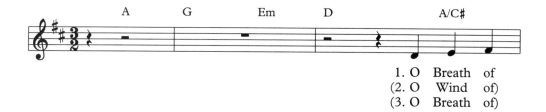

1. O Breath of
(2. O Wind of)
(3. O Breath of)

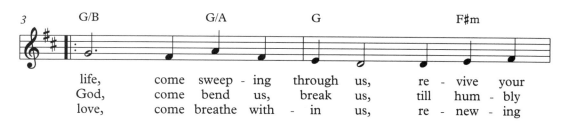

life,   come sweep - ing   through   us,   re - vive your
God,   come bend   us,   break   us,   till   hum - bly
love,   come breathe with - in   us,   re - new - ing

church with life and power. O Breath of   life,   come cleanse, re -
we   con - fess our need. Then in your ten - der - ness re -
thought and will and heart. Come, love of Christ, a - fresh to

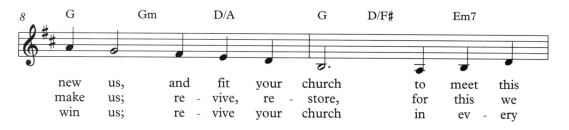

new   us,   and   fit   your church   to   meet this
make us;   re - vive, re - store,   for this   we
win   us;   re - vive your church   in   ev - ery

1, 2

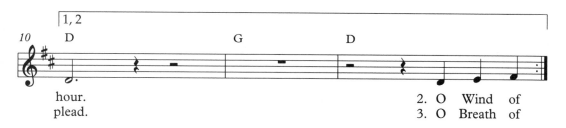

hour.   2. O Wind of
plead.   3. O Breath of

3   *rit.*

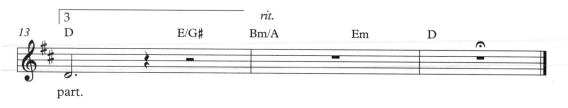

part.

WORDS: Bessie Porter Head
MUSIC: Carlton R. Young

ADIEU
98.98

3147

Built on a Rock

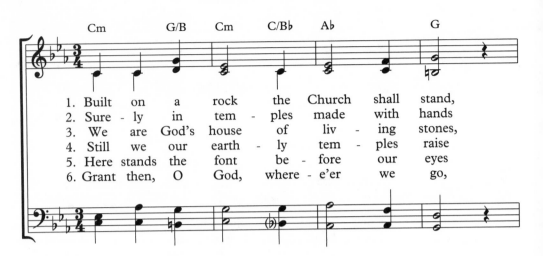

1. Built on a rock the Church shall stand,
2. Sure-ly in tem-ples made with hands
3. We are God's house of liv-ing stones,
4. Still we our earth-ly tem-ples raise
5. Here stands the font be-fore our eyes
6. Grant then, O God, where-e'er we go,

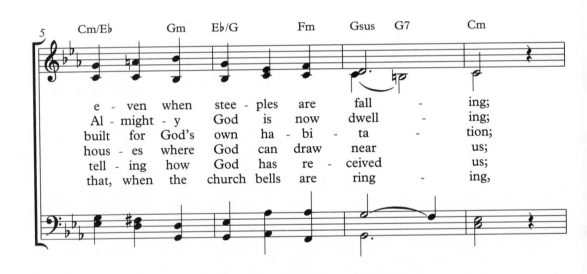

e-ven when stee-ples are fall - ing;
Al-might-y God is now dwell - ing;
built for God's own ha-bi-ta - tion;
hous-es where God can draw near us;
tell-ing how God has re-ceived us;
that, when the church bells are ring - ing,

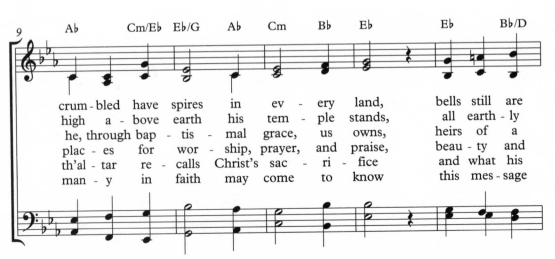

crum-bled have spires in ev-ery land,   bells still are
high a-bove earth his tem-ple stands,   all earth-ly
he, through bap-tis-mal grace, us owns,   heirs of a
plac-es for wor-ship, prayer, and praise, beau-ty and
th'al-tar re-calls Christ's sac-ri-fice   and what his
man-y in faith may come to know   this mes-sage

WORDS: Nikolai F. S. Grundtvig; trans. by Carl Doving; adapt. Dean McIntyre
MUSIC: Ludwig M. Lindeman

KIRKEN DEN ER ET GAMMELT HUS
88.88.88.8

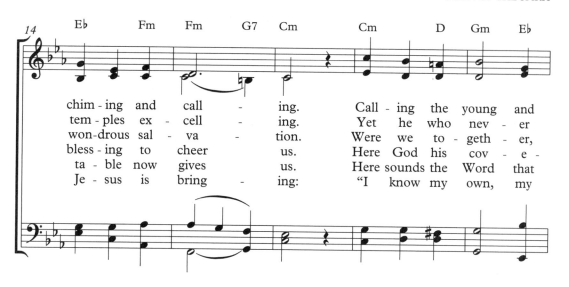

chim - ing and call - ing.
tem - ples ex - cell - ing.
won-drous sal - va - tion.
bless - ing to cheer us.
ta - ble now gives us.
Je - sus is bring - ing:

Call - ing the young and
Yet he who nev - er
Were we to - geth - er,
Here God his cov - e -
Here sounds the Word that
"I know my own, my

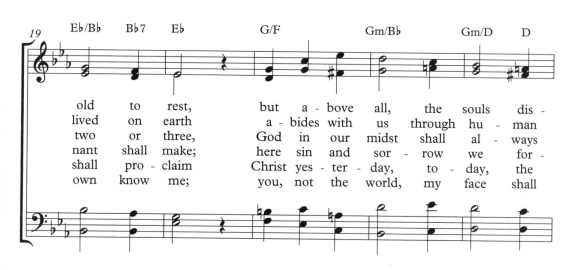

old to rest, but a - bove all, the souls dis -
lived on earth a - bides with us through hu - man
two or three, God in our midst shall al - ways
nant shall make; here sin and sor - row we for -
shall pro - claim Christ yes - ter - day, to - day, the
own know me; you, not the world, my face shall

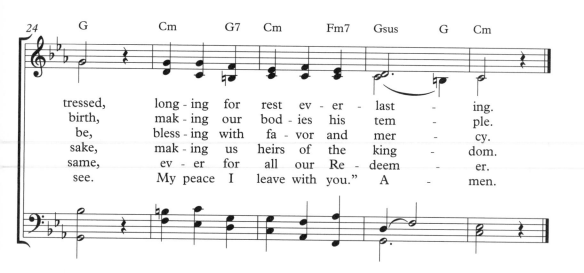

tressed, long - ing for rest ev - er - last - ing.
birth, mak - ing our bod - ies his tem - ple.
be, bless - ing with fa - vor and mer - cy.
sake, mak - ing us heirs of the king - dom.
same, ev - er for all our Re - deem - er.
see. My peace I leave with you." A - men.

3148   There's a Spirit of Love in This Place

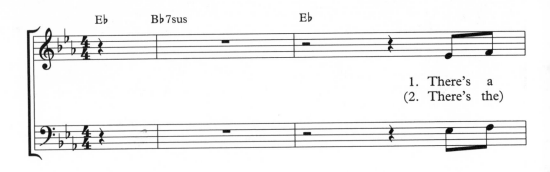

1. There's a
(2. There's the)

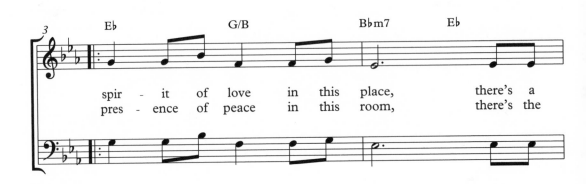

spir - it of love in this place, there's a
pres - ence of peace in this room, there's the

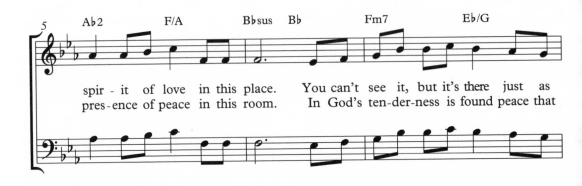

spir - it of love in this place. You can't see it, but it's there just as
pres - ence of peace in this room. In God's ten-der-ness is found peace that

pre - cious as the air. There's a spir - it of love in this
pass - es hu - man bounds. There's the pres - ence of peace in this

WORDS: Mark A. Miller
MUSIC: Mark A. Miller

MEDEMA
Irr.

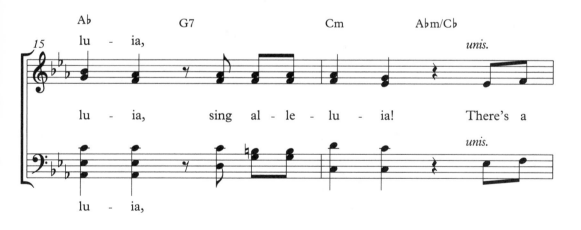

A Place at the Table

With energy! (♩ = 134-144)

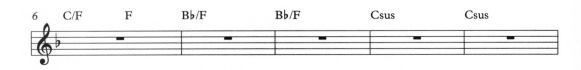

1. For ev - ery - one born, a
(2. For) wom - an and man, a
(3. For) young and for old, a
(4. For) just and un - just, a
(5. For) ev - ery - one born, a

Descant (Stanza 5 only)

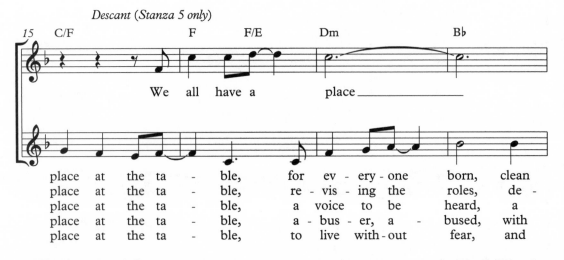

We all have a place

place at the ta - ble, for ev - ery - one born, clean
place at the ta - ble, re - vis - ing the roles, de-
place at the ta - ble, a voice to be heard, a
place at the ta - ble, a - bus - er, a - bused, with
place at the ta - ble, to live with - out fear, and

WORDS: Shirley Erena Murray
MUSIC: Lori True

PLACE AT THE TABLE
11 10.11 10 with Refrain

to live with-out fear._____

wa - ter and bread,_____ a shel - ter, a
cid - ing the share,_____ with wis - dom and
part in the song,_____ the hands of a
need to for - give,_____ in an - ger, in
sim - ply to be,_____ to work, to speak

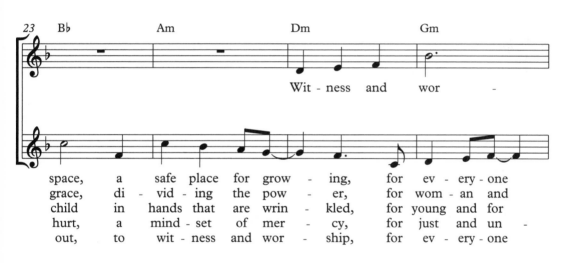

Wit - ness and wor -

space, a safe place for grow - ing, for ev - ery-one
grace, di - vid - ing the pow - er, for wom - an and
child in hands that are wrin - kled, for young and for
hurt, a mind - set of mer - cy, for just and un -
out, to wit - ness and wor - ship, for ev - ery-one

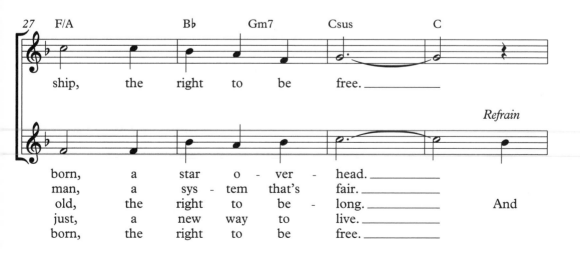

Refrain

ship, the right to be free._____

born, a star o - ver - head._____
man, a sys - tem that's fair._____
old, the right to be - long._____ And
just, a new way to live._____
born, the right to be free._____

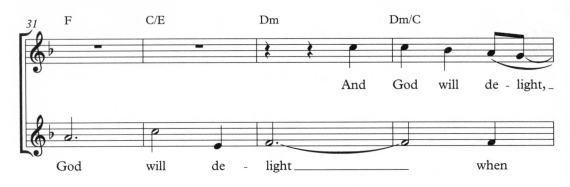

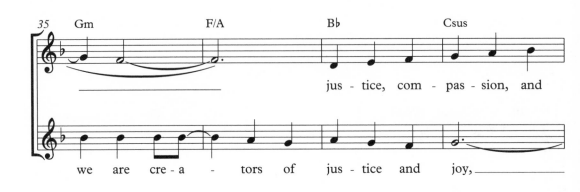

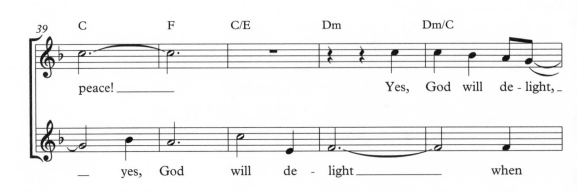

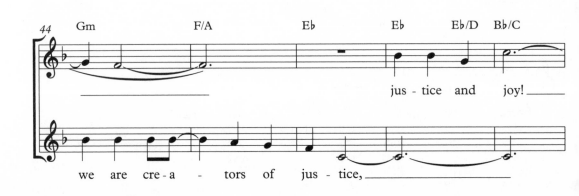

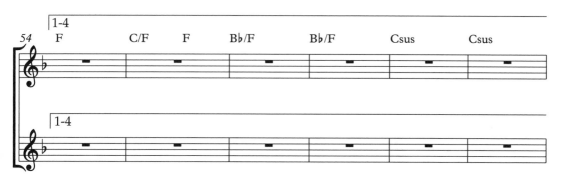

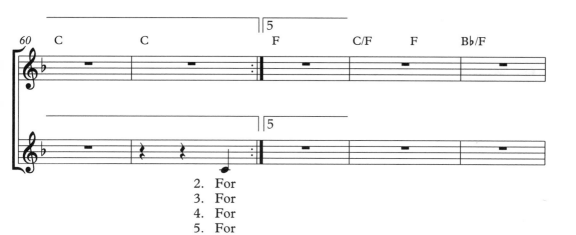

2. For
3. For
4. For
5. For

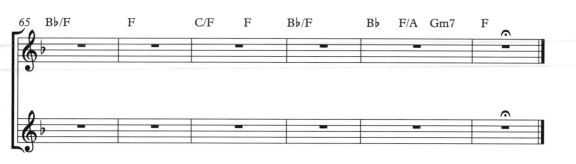

3150 Father, We Have Heard You Calling

4 vs.

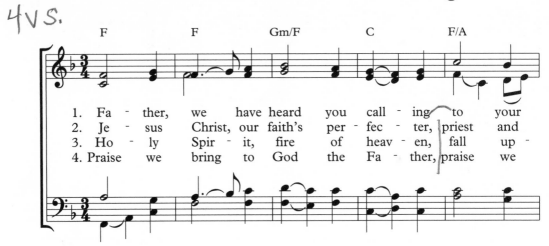

1. Fa - ther, we have heard you call - ing to your
2. Je - sus Christ, our faith's per - fec - ter, priest and
3. Ho - ly Spir - it, fire of heav - en, fall up -
4. Praise we bring to God the Fa - ther, praise we

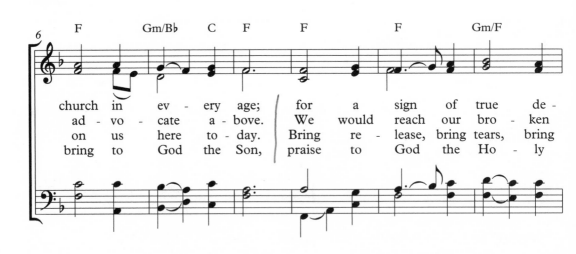

church in ev - ery age; for a sign of true de -
ad - vo - cate a - bove. We would reach our bro - ken
on us here to - day. Bring re - lease, bring tears, bring
bring to God the Son, praise to God the Ho - ly

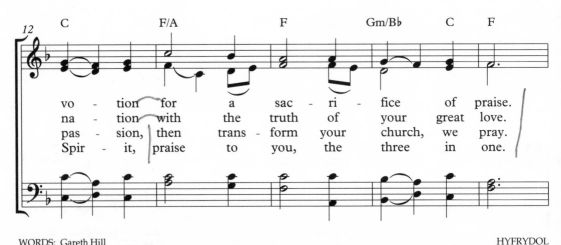

vo - tion for a sac - ri - fice of praise.
na - tion with the truth of your great love.
pas - sion, then trans - form your church, we pray.
Spir - it, praise to you, the three in one.

WORDS: Gareth Hill
MUSIC: Rowland H. Prichard; harm. from *The English Hymnal*
Words © 2005 Hope Publishing Company

HYFRYDOL
87.87 D

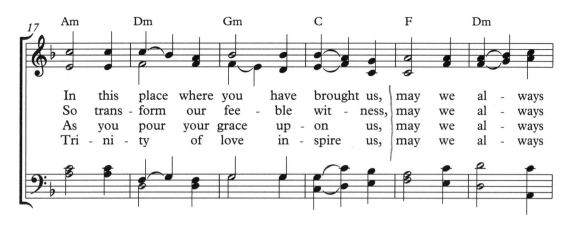

In this place where you have brought us, may we al - ways
So trans - form our fee - ble wit - ness, may we al - ways
As you pour your grace up - on us, may we al - ways
Tri - ni - ty of love in - spire us, may we al - ways

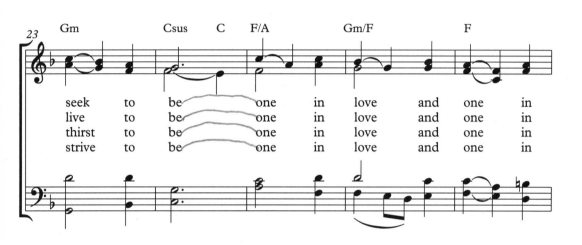

seek to be one in love and one in
live to be one in love and one in
thirst to be one in love and one in
strive to be one in love and one in

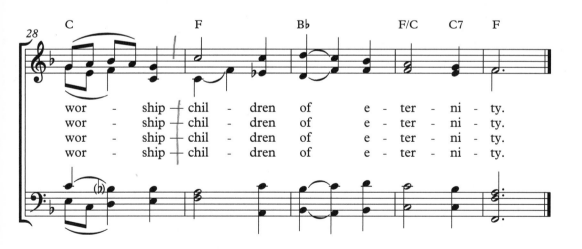

wor - ship chil - dren of e - ter - ni - ty.
wor - ship chil - dren of e - ter - ni - ty.
wor - ship chil - dren of e - ter - ni - ty.
wor - ship chil - dren of e - ter - ni - ty.

3151

The Jesus in Me

Moderately

The Je - sus in me loves the
El Je - sus en mi al - ma el

Je - sus in you, the Je - sus in me loves the Je - sus in you, so eas-
Je - sus en ti, El Je - sus en mi al - ma el Je - sus en ti tan fa-

y, so eas - y, so eas-
cil, tan fa - cil, tan fa-

y, so eas - y to love. _____
cil, tan fa - cil a - mor. _____

WORDS: Anonymous
MUSIC: Anonymous, arr. by Cynthia Wilson

SO EASY
Irr.

3152

Welcome

1. Let's walk to - geth - er
(2. Let's) talk to - geth - er
(3. Let's) dream to - geth - er

WORDS: Laurie Zelman and Mark A. Miller
MUSIC: Mark A. Miller

WELCOME
Irr. with Refrain

for a while and ask where we be - gin ___ to
of a time when we will share a feast, __ where
of the day when earth and heaven are one, __ a

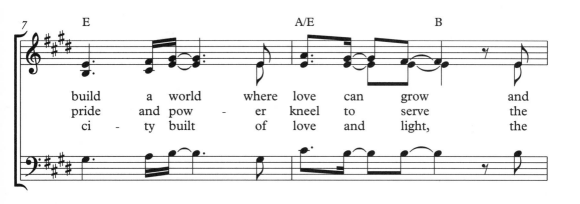

build a world where love can grow and
pride and pow - er kneel to serve and the
ci - ty built of love and light, the

hope can en - ter in, ___ ___ to be the hands of
lone - ly and the least, _ ___ and joy will set the
new Je - ru - sa - lem, __ where our mourn - ing turns to

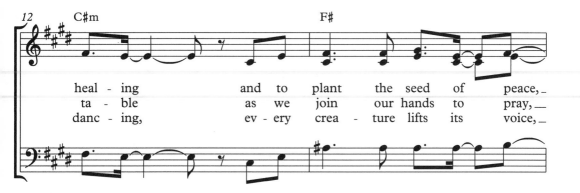

heal - ing and to plant the seed of peace, _
ta - ble as we join our hands to pray, __
danc - ing, ev - ery crea - ture lifts its voice, _

O God, in Whom We Live

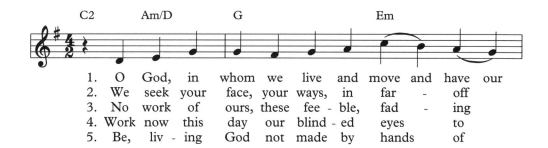

1. O God, in whom we live and move and have our
2. We seek your face, your ways, in far - off
3. No work of ours, these fee - ble, fad - ing
4. Work now this day our blind - ed eyes to
5. Be, liv - ing God not made by hands of

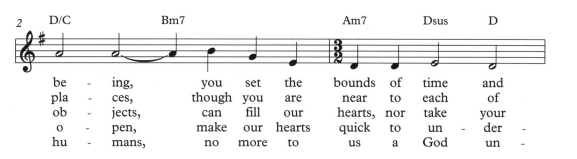

be - ing, you set the bounds of time and
pla - ces, though you are near to each of
ob - jects, can fill our hearts, nor take your
o - pen, make our hearts quick to un - der -
hu - mans, no more to us a God un -

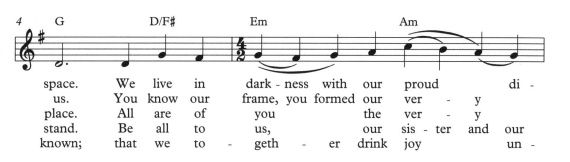

space. We live in dark - ness with our proud di -
us. You know our frame, you formed our ver - y
place. All are of you the ver - y
stand. Be all to us, our sis - ter and our
known; that we to - geth - er drink joy un -

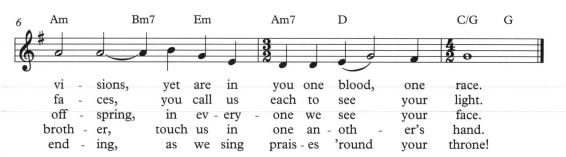

vi - sions, yet are in you one blood, one race.
fa - ces, you call us each to see your light.
off - spring, in ev - ery - one we see your face.
broth - er, touch us in one an - oth - er's hand.
end - ing, as we sing prais - es 'round your throne!

WORDS: William P. Gorton
MUSIC: William P. Gorton
© 2007 William P. Gorton

AREOPAGUS
Irr.

3154

Draw the Circle Wide

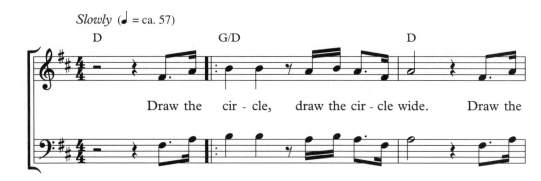

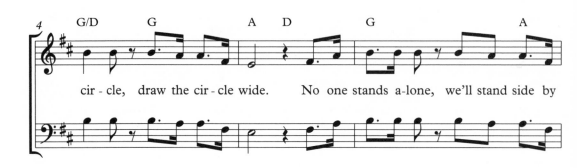

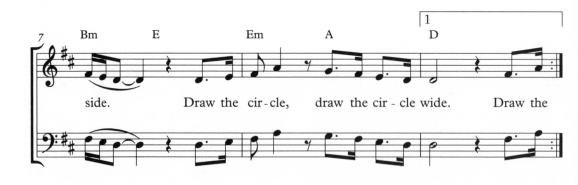

WORDS: Gordon Light
MUSIC: Mark A. Miller

DRAW THE CIRCLE
Irr.

The Lord of Life, a Vine Is He

3155

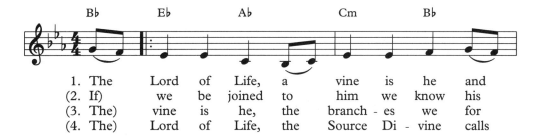

1. The Lord of Life, a vine is he and
(2.) If we be joined to him we know his
(3.) The vine is he, the branch- es we for
(4.) The Lord of Life, the Source Di - vine calls

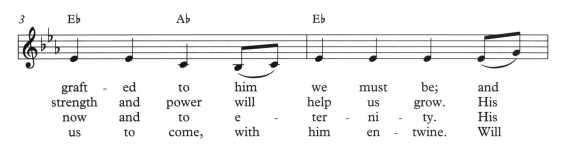

graft - ed to him we must be; and
strength and power will help us grow. His
now and to e - ter - ni - ty. His
us to come, with him en - twine. Will

thus we yield a - bun- dant- ly sweet fruit for all to
Spir- it's grace through us will flow to prune and shape us
word sown deep in us will be both sun and rain... suf-
we, un - hear- ing, dare de - cline the call of Christ, the

taste and see. 2. If
as we go. 3. The
fi - cien - cy 4. The
One True Vine?

WORDS: Mary Kay Beall
MUSIC: John Carter
LATHAM
LM

3156 One Is the Body

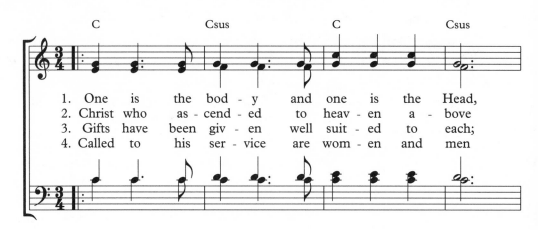

1. One is the bod-y and one is the Head,
2. Christ who as-cend-ed to heav-en a-bove
3. Gifts have been giv-en well suit-ed to each;
4. Called to his ser-vice are wom-en and men

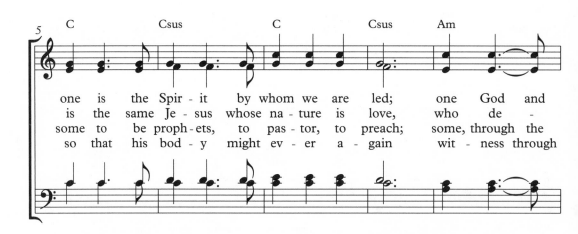

one is the Spir-it by whom we are led; one God and
is the same Je-sus whose na-ture is love, who de-
some to be proph-ets, to pas-tor, to preach; some, through the
so that his bod-y might ev-er a-gain wit-ness through

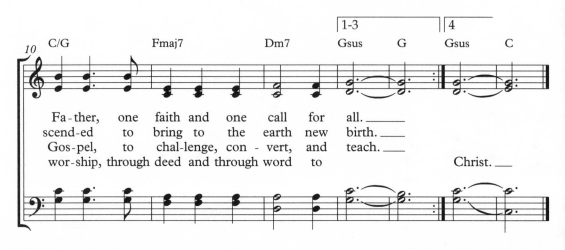

Fa-ther, one faith and one call for all. _____
scend-ed to bring to the earth new birth. _____
Gos-pel, to chal-lenge, con-vert, and teach. _____
wor-ship, through deed and through word to Christ. _____

WORDS: John Bell
MUSIC: John Bell

ONE IS THE BODY
Irr.

Come, Let Us Dream

3157

1. Come, let us dream God's dream a-gain. Come, one and
2. The lame shall walk, the blind shall see, the doors swing
3. When ha-tred ends and war shall cease, so all may
4. But know the cost of claim-ing sight of God's new
5. Proph-ets are scorned in their own lands and mar-tyrs

all, let us as-cend the moun-tain-top where those of
wide, all pri-soners free, the low-ly raised, the proud brought
dwell in deep-est peace, then be as-sured the time is
day, of wrongs made right, for some have paid the high-est
slain by righ-teous hands; though dream-ers die, the dream will

old saw God's new day on earth un-fold.
low. This is God's dream: let jus-tice flow.
near when per-fect love casts out all fear.
price, their lives for us, a sac-ri-fice.
live, for we have yet our lives to give.

WORDS: John Middleton
MUSIC: English folk melody; harm. by Dean McIntyre

O WALY WALY
LM

3158

Go to the World

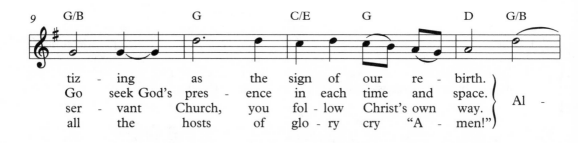

1. Go to the world! Go in-to all the earth. Go
2. Go to the world! Go in-to ev-ery place. Go
3. Go to the world! Go strug-gle, bless and pray; the
4. Go to the world! Go as the ones I send, for

preach the cross where Christ's re-news life's worth, bap-
Go live the Word of God's re-deem-ing grace. Go
nights of tears give way to joy-ous day. As
I am with you 'til the age shall end, when

tiz - ing as the sign of our re - birth.
Go seek God's pres - ence in each time and space.
ser - vant Church, you fol-low Christ's own way.
all the hosts of glo - ry cry "A - men!"

Al - le - lu - ia. Al - le - lu - ia.

WORDS: Sylvia G. Dunstan
MUSIC: Ralph Vaughan Williams
Words © 1991 GIA Publications, Inc.

SINE NOMINE
10 10 10 with Alleluias

Let Our Earth Be Peaceful

3159

1. Let our earth be peace-ful, let our hearts be
2. Let our ways be mind-ful, mend-ing what is
3. Let our lives be fruit-ful, beau-ti-ful and

hope - ful, let our hands be gen - tle
hurt - ful, do - ing what is need - ful
play - ful, ev - ery day be thank - ful

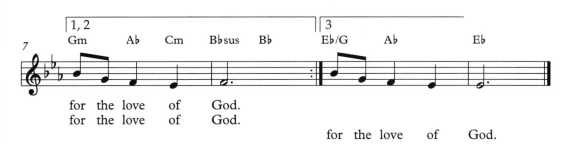

for the love of God.
for the love of God.

for the love of God.

WORDS: Shirley Erena Murray
MUSIC: Carlton R. Young

RAYMOND
66.65

3160

We Will Follow
(Somlandela)

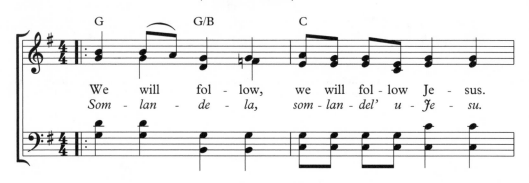

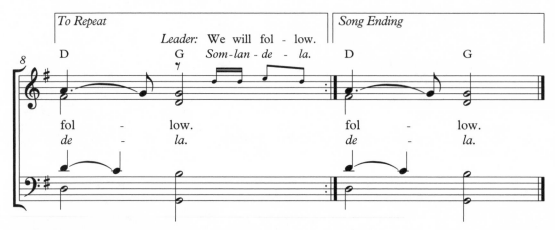

WORDS: Traditional Zulu
MUSIC: Traditional Zulu; arr. by Dean McIntyre

SOMLANDELA
10 9.10 10

Gracious Creator of Sea and of Land   3161

($\quad$ = 90)

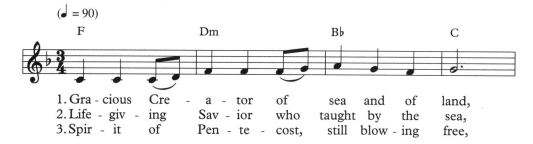

1. Gra - cious Cre - a - tor of sea and of land,
2. Life - giv - ing Sav - ior who taught by the sea,
3. Spir - it of Pen - te - cost, still blow - ing free,

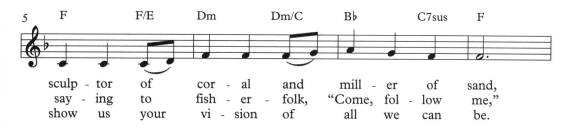

sculp - tor of cor - al and mill - er of sand,
say - ing to fish - er - folk, "Come, fol - low me,"
show us your vi - sion of all we can be.

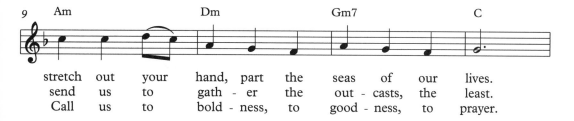

stretch out your hand, part the seas of our lives.
send us to gath - er the out - casts, the least.
Call us to bold - ness, to good - ness, to prayer.

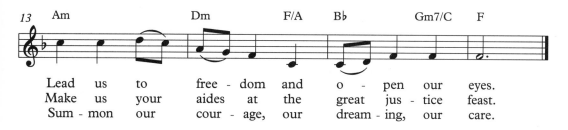

Lead us to free - dom and o - pen our eyes.
Make us your aides at the great jus - tice feast.
Sum - mon our cour - age, our dream - ing, our care.

WORDS: John Thornburg
MUSIC: Daniel Charles Damon

MONA WEST
10 10.10 10

3162 Stand in Awe

WORDS: Psalm 22:22-30, adapt. by Bret Hesla
MUSIC: Bret Hesla

© 2006 Augsburg Fortress

STAND IN AWE
13 10.13 9

3163 Walking in the Light of God

Refrain

Walk in the light, walk in the light,

To Stanzas
Last time - Fine

walk in the light, walk-ing in the light of God.

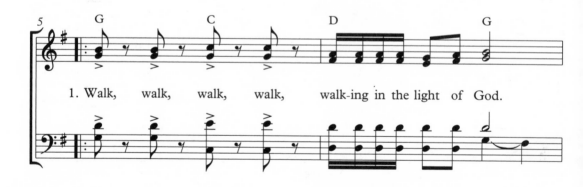

1. Walk, walk, walk, walk, walk-ing in the light of God.

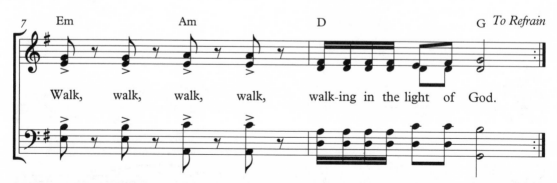

To Refrain

Walk, walk, walk, walk, walk-ing in the light of God.

WORDS: Traditional Zulu
MUSIC: Traditional Zulu; arr. by Dean McIntyre

HAMBA
Irr. with Refrain

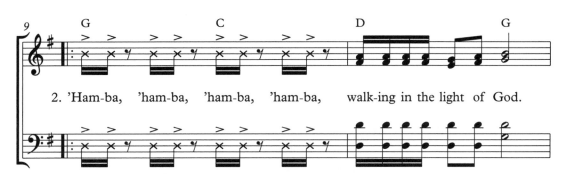

2. 'Ham-ba, 'ham-ba, 'ham-ba, 'ham-ba, walk-ing in the light of God.

To Refrain

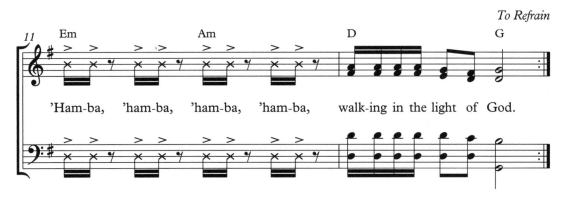

'Ham-ba, 'ham-ba, 'ham-ba, 'ham-ba, walk-ing in the light of God.

3. 'Ham - ba koo kah nigh nee, 'ham - ba koo kah nigh nee,

To Refrain

'ham - ba koo kah nigh nee, walk-ing in the light of God.

3164 Down to the River to Pray

* 2. brothers
  3. fathers
  4. mothers
  5. sinners

WORDS: Southern USA folk song
MUSIC: Southern USA folk song; transcribed by Jackson Henry

Transcription © 2011 Jackson Henry

DOWN TO THE RIVER
Irr.

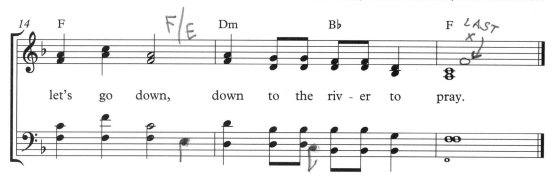

let's go down, down to the riv - er to pray.

Take Me to the Water

3165

1. Take me to the wa - ter. Take me to the wa -
2. None but the right - eous, none but the right -
3. I love Je - sus, I love Je -
4. He's my Sav - ior. He's my Sav -

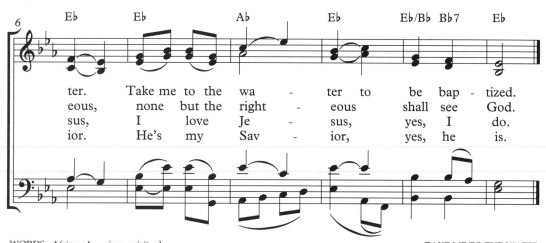

ter. Take me to the wa - ter to be bap - tized.
eous, none but the right - eous shall see God.
sus, I love Je - sus, yes, I do.
ior. He's my Sav - ior, yes, he is.

WORDS: African American spiritual
MUSIC: African American spiritual

TAKE ME TO THE WATER
Irr.

3166 Author of Life Divine

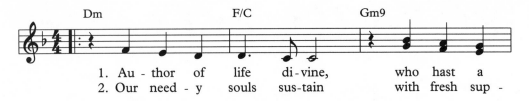

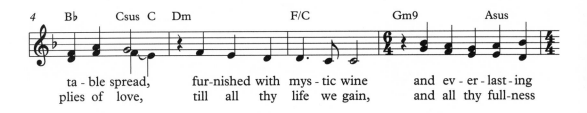

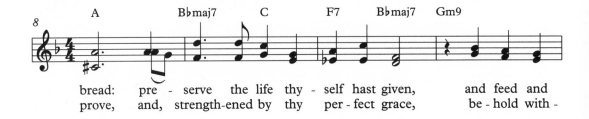

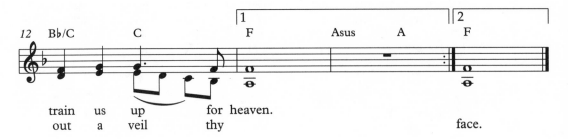

1. Au-thor of life di-vine, who hast a ta-ble spread, fur-nished with mys-tic wine and ev-er-last-ing bread: pre-serve the life thy-self hast given, and feed and train us up for heaven.

2. Our need-y souls sus-tain with fresh sup-plies of love, till all thy life we gain, and all thy full-ness prove, and, strength-ened by thy per-fect grace, be-hold with-out a veil thy face.

WORDS: Charles Wesley
MUSIC: Jackson Henry
Music © 2009 Jackson Henry

AUTHOR
66.66.88

3167 Feed Us, Lord

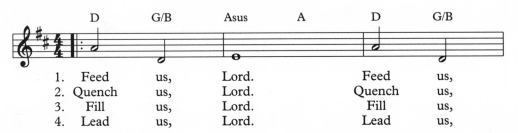

1. Feed us, Lord. Feed us,
2. Quench us, Lord. Quench us,
3. Fill us, Lord. Fill us,
4. Lead us, Lord. Lead us,

WORDS: Greg Scheer
MUSIC: Greg Scheer
© 2007 Greg Scheer

FEED US
33.55.7

Lord. In the bro-ken bread, be re-vealed a-gain. Come and
Lord. On this thirst-y ground, may your love flow down. Come and
Lord, with the bread and wine of the ris-en Christ. Come and
Lord. Nour-ished here by Christ; giv-en strength for life. Come and

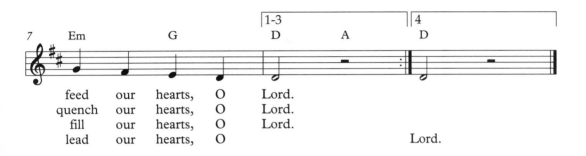

feed our hearts, O Lord.
quench our hearts, O Lord.
fill our hearts, O Lord.
lead our hearts, O Lord.

Come to the Table of Grace 3168

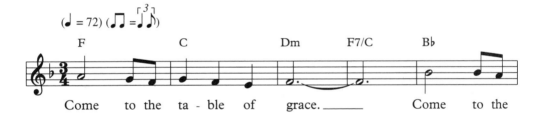

Come to the ta-ble of grace._____ Come to the

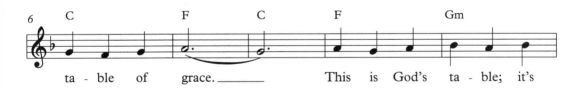

ta-ble of grace._____ This is God's ta-ble; it's

not yours or mine. Come to the ta-ble of grace._____

2. Come to the table of peace...
3. Come to the table of love...
4. Come to the table of joy...

WORDS: Barbara Hamm
MUSIC: Barbara Hamm
© 2008 Barbara Hamm

TABLE OF GRACE
7 7.10 7

3169 You Feed Us, Gentle Savior

1. You feed us, gen-tle Sav - ior, the bread that makes us whole,
2. You bind us, gen-tle Sav - ior, and weave us in - to one,
3. You call us, gen-tle Sav - ior, and send us in your name.

the wine of your com - pas - sion poured out in - to our soul.
one flesh and blood made ho - ly, the Bod - y of your Son.
You teach and heal and show us how we can do the same.

The food of your own pres - ence, your Spir - it, strong, with - in,
We gath - er here in hun - ger, one hun - ger, all the same;
So, strength-ened by your Spir - it and nour-ished by your grace,

the grace that heals us deep - ly and o - ver-comes our sin.
and with one grace you bless us to - geth - er in his name.
we go to be your pres - ence in love, in ev - ery place.

WORDS: Steve Garnaas-Holmes
MUSIC: Hal H. Hopson

MERLE'S TUNE
76.76 D

Words © 2009 Steve Garnaas-Holmes; music © 1983 Hope Publishing Company

3170 What Feast of Love

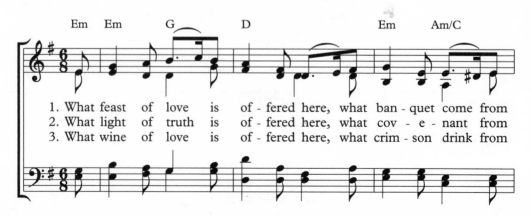

1. What feast of love is of - fered here, what ban - quet come from
2. What light of truth is of - fered here, what cov - e - nant from
3. What wine of love is of - fered here, what crim - son drink from

WORDS: Delores Dufner
MUSIC: English melody, 16th cent.

GREENSLEEVES
87.87.67.67

Words © 1993 Delores Dufner, OSB, admin. OCP Publications

3171-a   Communion Setting
(Sanctus and Benedictus)

WORDS: From *The United Methodist Hymnal*
MUSIC: Sally Ahner

SANCTUS (AHNER)
Irr.

Music © 1983 Sally Ahner

3171-b   (Memorial Acclamation)

WORDS: From *The United Methodist Hymnal*
MUSIC: Sally Ahner

ACCLAMATION (AHNER)
Irr.

Music © 1983 Sally Ahner

3171-c   (Amen)

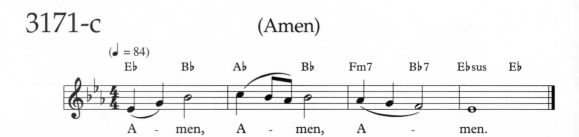

WORDS: From *The United Methodist Hymnal*
MUSIC: Sally Ahner

AMEN (AHNER)
Irr.

Music © 1988, 1996 Sally Ahner

Communion Setting
(Holy, Holy, Holy)

3172-a

WORDS: From *The United Methodist Hymnal*
MUSIC: Jackson Henry

SANCTUS (HENRY)
Irr.

3172-b   (Christt Has Died)

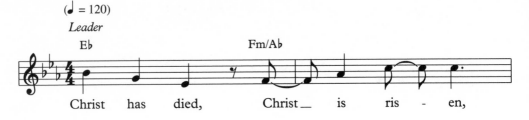

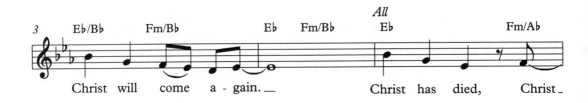

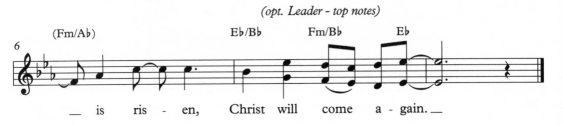

WORDS: From *The United Methodist Hymnal*
MUSIC: Jackson Henry

Music © 2011 Jackson Henry

ACCLAMATION (HENRY)
Irr.

3172-c   (Amen)

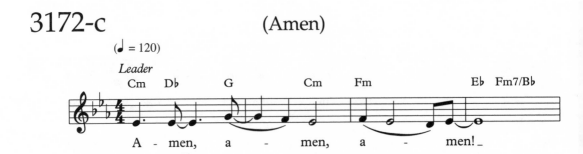

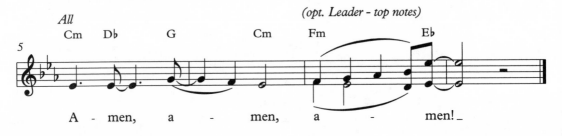

WORDS: From *The United Methodist Hymnal*
MUSIC: Jackson Henry

Music © 2011 Jackson Henry

AMEN (HENRY)
Irr.

Table of Plenty

3173

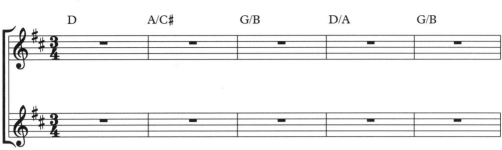

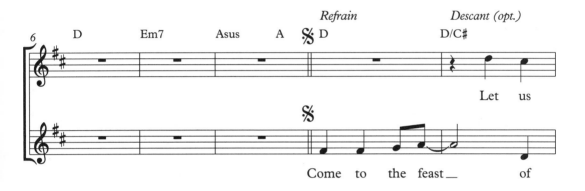

WORDS: Dan Schutte
MUSIC: Dan Schutte
© 1992 Daniel L. Schutte

PLENTY
Irr. with Refrain

vide what we need here at the ta - ble of

all that we need here at the ta - ble of

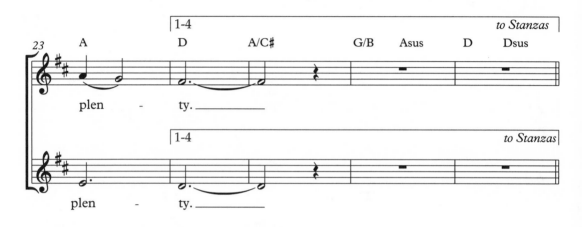

plen - ty.

plen - ty.

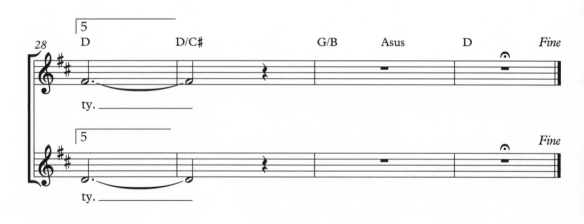

ty.

ty.

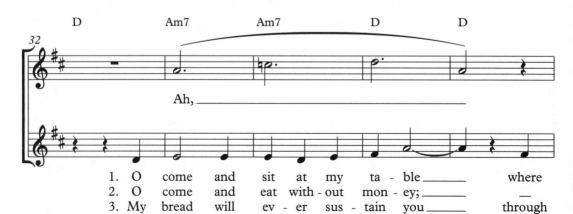

Ah,

1. O come and sit at my ta - ble _____ where
2. O come and eat with - out mon - ey; _____ —
3. My bread will ev - er sus - tain you _____ through
4. Your fields will flow - er in full - ness; _____ your

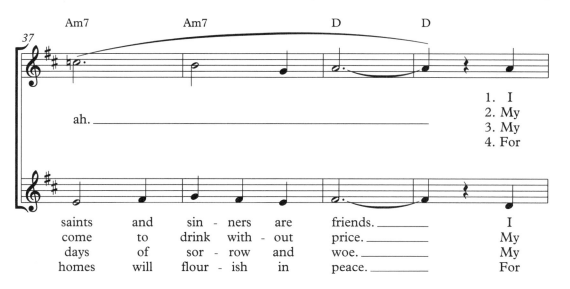

Am7   Am7   D   D

ah. _____

1. I
2. My
3. My
4. For

saints   and   sin - ners   are   friends. _____   I
come   to   drink   with - out   price. _____   My
days   of   sor - row   and   woe. _____   My
homes   will   flour - ish   in   peace. _____   For

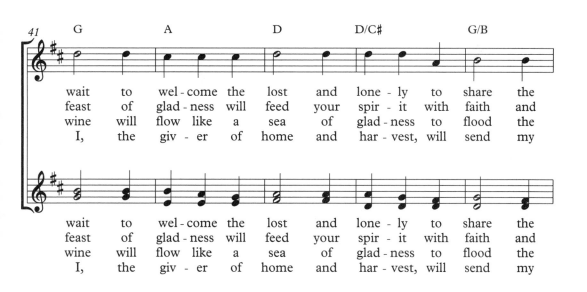

G   A   D   D/C♯   G/B

wait   to   wel - come   the   lost   and   lone - ly   to   share   the
feast   of   glad - ness   will   feed   your   spir - it   with   faith   and
wine   will   flow   like   a   sea   of   glad - ness   to   flood   the
I,   the   giv - er   of   home   and   har - vest,   will   send   my

wait   to   wel - come   the   lost   and   lone - ly   to   share   the
feast   of   glad - ness   will   feed   your   spir - it   with   faith   and
wine   will   flow   like   a   sea   of   glad - ness   to   flood   the
I,   the   giv - er   of   home   and   har - vest,   will   send   my

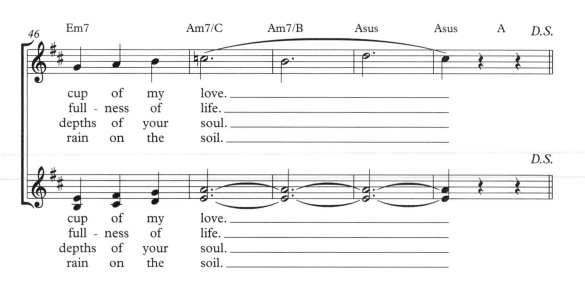

Em7   Am7/C   Am7/B   Asus   Asus   A   D.S.

cup   of   my   love. _____
full - ness   of   life. _____
depths   of   your   soul. _____
rain   on   the   soil. _____

D.S.

cup   of   my   love. _____
full - ness   of   life. _____
depths   of   your   soul. _____
rain   on   the   soil. _____

3174 Christ, We Are Blest

1. Christ, we are blest as we gath-er to dine,
2. You laid your life down like sow-ing a seed;
3. Christ, you are ris-en, but not far a-bove:
4. Je-sus, you feed us, then bid us to leave,

strength-ened for love by the bread and the wine.
once dead and bur-ied, from death you are freed,
you live a-mong us in each act of love,
shar-ing with oth-ers the love we re-ceive.

This is your bod-y, now en-ter-ing ours,
ris-ing like wheat in the warmth of the sun!
in ev-ery deed of com-pas-sion you rise,
We are your bod-y, sent by your com-mand,

strong with your lov-ing mi-rac-u-lous powers.
Christ, you are ris-en! New life has be-gun!
liv-ing in flesh we can see with our eyes.
mak-ing love real as the bread in our hands.

WORDS: Steve Garnaas-Holmes
MUSIC: Irish folk melody; harm. by Carlton R. Young

SLANE
10 10.10 10

Words © 2009, harm. © 1964 Abingdon Press, admin. by The Copyright Company

Christ, We Come with Joy and Gladness 3175

1. Christ, we come with joy and glad-ness as we wit-ness love made new;
2. Hope and joy and love a-bound-ing, this our prayer for their suc-cess;

hear the prayers of two u-nit-ed as their lives are joined in you.
let the lives of these, our loved ones, know the joy of those you bless.

Seek-ing you to bond their mar-riage, they are trust-ing you to be in __
Christ, our Shep-herd, tend and keep them, and your peace and care be known. May __

__ the cord that can't be bro-ken, giv-ing them the strength of three.
__ the world in which you place them praise you as their love is shown.

WORDS: Constance M. Cherry
MUSIC: Ludwig van Beethoven; arr. by Edward Hodges

HYMN TO JOY
87.87D

3176 Come, Now Is the Time to Worship

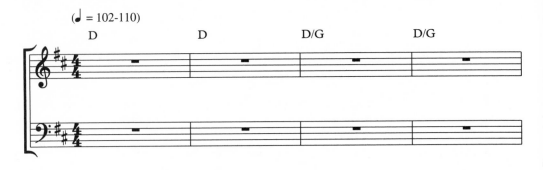

Come, now is the time to wor - ship. _

Come, now is the time to give _ your heart. _

Come, just as you are to wor - ship. _

WORDS: Brian Doerksen
MUSIC: Brian Doerksen

NOW IS THE TIME
Irr.

Last time to Coda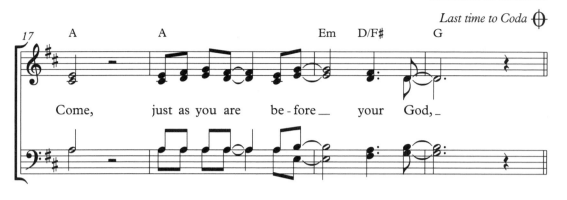

come, just as you are be-fore __ your God, __

come. One day ev-ery tongue will con-fess __

__ you are God. One day ev-ery knee will bow. __

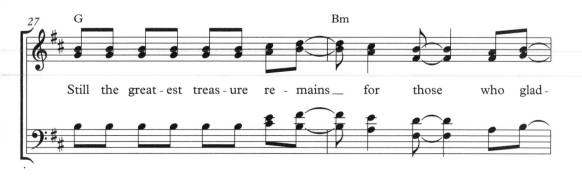

Still the great-est treas-ure re-mains __ for those who glad-

ly   choose   you   now. __

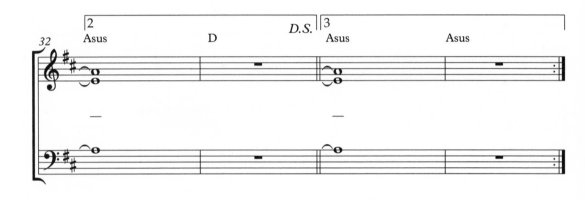

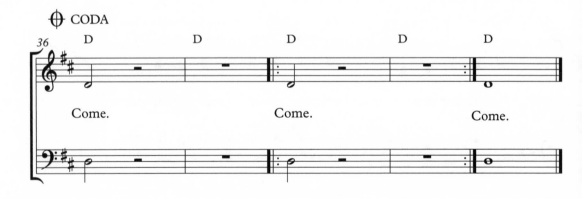

Come.   Come.   Come.

Here I Am to Worship

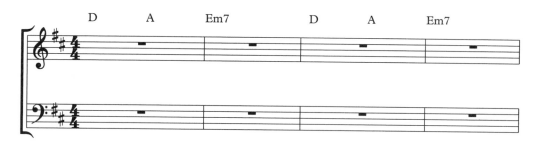

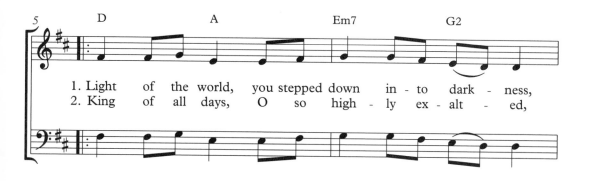

1. Light of the world, you stepped down in-to dark - ness,
2. King of all days, O so high - ly ex - alt - ed,

o - pened my eyes, let me see. Beau - ty that made this
glo - rious in heav - en a - bove. Hum - bly you came to the

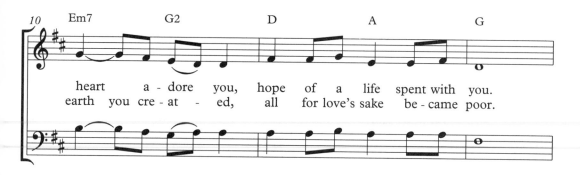

heart a - dore you, hope of a life spent with you.
earth you cre - at - ed, all for love's sake be - came poor.

WORDS: Tim Hughes
MUSIC: Tim Hughes

HERE I AM TO WORSHIP
Irr.

3178 Lord, You Are Welcome

Refrain

Lord, you are wel-come, you're wel-come, you are

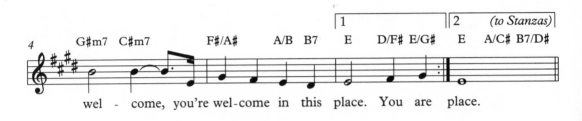

wel-come, you're wel-come in this place. You are place.

place. Lord, our ho-ly hands we raise to

wor-ship and give you praise. We in-voke your ho-ly

pres-ence, O Lord, to come and fill this place.

WORDS: Warren Jones
MUSIC: Warren Jones; arr. by Nolan Williams, Jr.

© 2000 GIA Publications, Inc.

YOU ARE WELCOME
Irr.

The Risen Christ

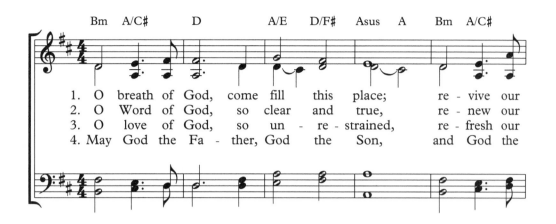

1. O breath of God, come fill this place; re - vive our
2. O Word of God, so clear and true, re - new our
3. O love of God, so un - re - strained, re - fresh our
4. May God the Fa - ther, God the Son, and God the

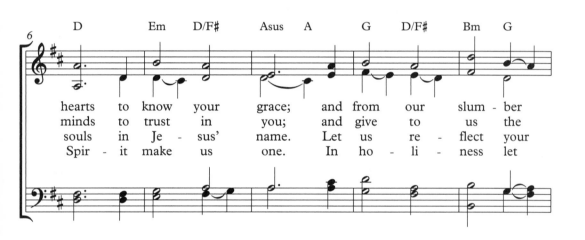

hearts to know your grace; and from our slum - ber
minds to trust in you; and give to us the
souls in Je - sus' name. Let us re - flect your
Spir - it make us one. In ho - li - ness let

make us rise that we may know the ris - en Christ.
bread of life that we may know the ris - en Christ.
sac - ri - fice that we may know the ris - en Christ.
us u - nite that we may know the ris - en Christ.

WORDS: Keith Getty and Phil Madeira
MUSIC: Keith Getty and Phil Madeira; arr. by Bruce Greer

THE RISEN CHRIST
LM

3180 As We Part for the Towns and Cities

WORDS: John Thornburg
MUSIC: Jackson Henry

CONNECTION
Irr.

Peace, Salaam, Shalom

3181

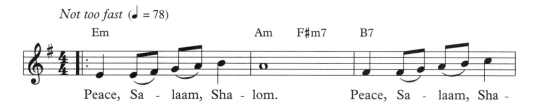

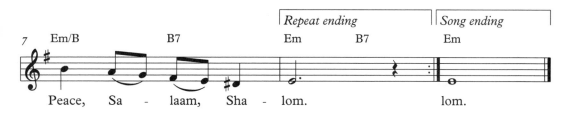

WORDS: Traditional
MUSIC: Dean McIntyre

BEERSHEBA
55.55

3182 Benediction Hymn

O Lord, now let your ser-vants de-part in peace, ac-cord-ing

to your gra-cious word. Our eyes have seen the glo-ry of sal-

va-tion pre-pared for all the peo-ple of the

world. Now may the Lord bless you and keep you and make his

WORDS: Luke 2:28-32; Numbers 6:24-26
MUSIC: Traditional Irish melody; transcription by Dean McIntyre

LONDONDERRY AIR
Irr.

As We Go   3183

WORDS: Jeremy Johnson
MUSIC: Jeremy Johnson; arr. David Shipps

AS WE GO
Irr.

3184

Word of God, Speak

1. I'm find-ing my - self
(2. I'm find-ing my - self)

at a loss for words, and the
in the midst of you, be-yond the

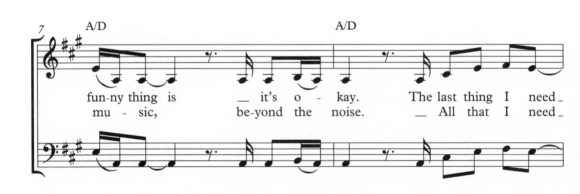

fun-ny thing is it's o - kay. The last thing I need
mu - sic, be-yond the noise. All that I need

is to be heard, but to hear what you would
is to be with You, and in the qui - et, I hear your

say.
voice. Word of God, speak. _ Would you pour down like rain, –

_ wash - ing my eyes _ to see your maj -

es - ty, to be still and know _ that you're in this place? _

Third time to Coda

_ Please let me stay _ and rest in your ho -

Send Us Your Spirit

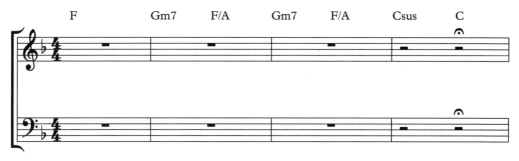

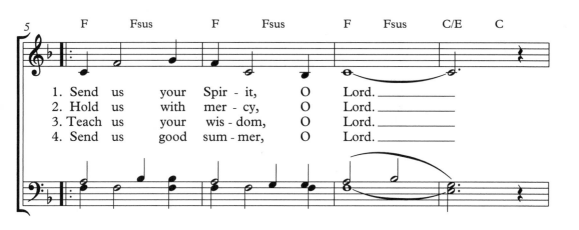

1. Send us your Spir - it, O Lord.
2. Hold us with mer - cy, O Lord.
3. Teach us your wis - dom, O Lord.
4. Send us good sum - mer, O Lord.

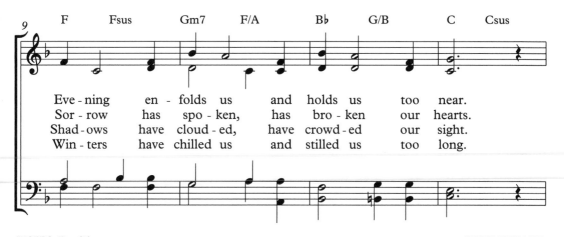

Eve - ning en - folds us and holds us too near.
Sor - row has spo - ken, has bro - ken our hearts.
Shad - ows have cloud - ed, have crowd - ed our sight.
Win - ters have chilled us and stilled us too long.

WORDS: Dan Schutte
MUSIC: Dan Schutte

EVENING PRAYER
7 10.10 7

13

A/C♯ · A7 · Dm · B♭ · C/B♭

Wake the morn-ing light. Make our liv-ing
Clothe us in your care. Be the life we
Give us hearts that see. Set our lov-ing
Give us love's own fire. Be our true de-

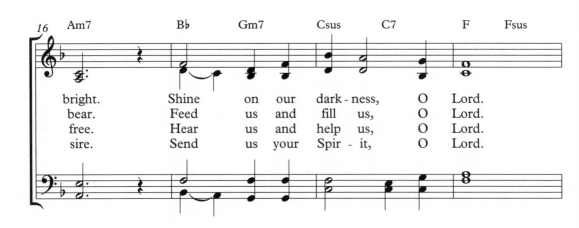

16

Am7 · B♭ · Gm7 · Csus · C7 · F · Fsus

bright. Shine on our dark-ness, O Lord.
bear. Feed us and fill us, O Lord.
free. Hear us and help us, O Lord.
sire. Send us your Spir-it, O Lord.

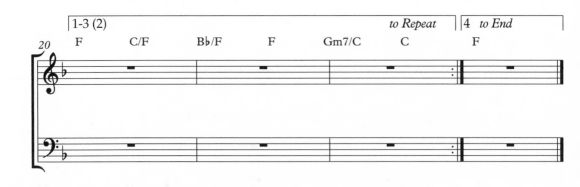

1-3 (2) · to Repeat · 4 to End

20

F · C/F · B♭/F · F · Gm7/C · C · F

3 Optional modulation (stanza 4)

24

A♭/E♭ · E♭ · A♭ · A♭sus · A♭ · A♭sus

4. Send us good sum-mer, O

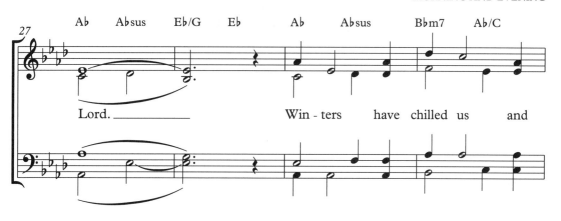

Lord. _____ Win - ters have chilled us and

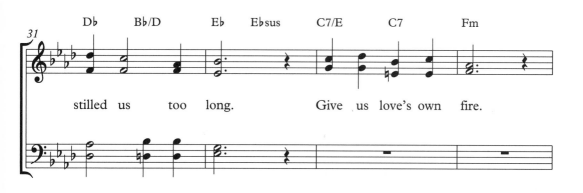

stilled us too long. Give us love's own fire.

Be our true de - sire. Send us your Spir - it, O

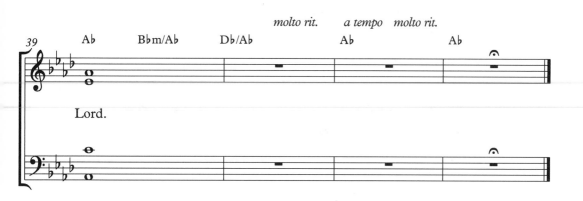

Lord.

Days of Elijah

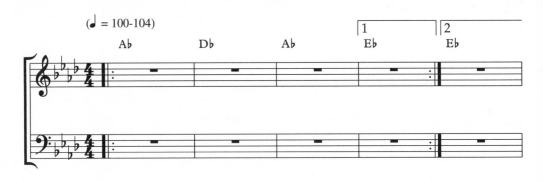

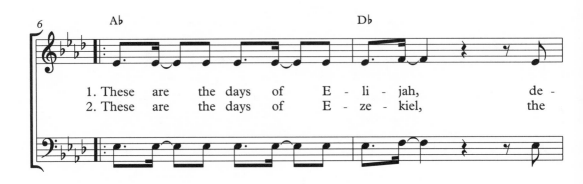

1. These are the days of E-li-jah, de-
2. These are the days of E-ze-kiel, the

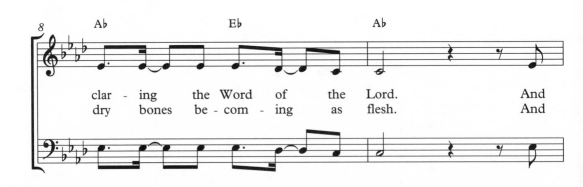

clar-ing the Word of the Lord. And
dry bones be-com-ing as flesh. And

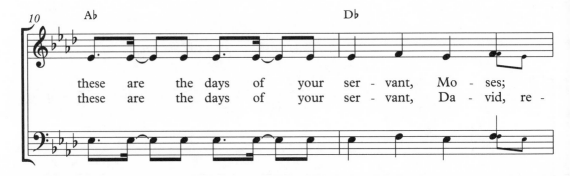

these are the days of your ser-vant, Mo-ses;
these are the days of your ser-vant, Da-vid, re-

WORDS: Robin Mark
MUSIC: Robin Mark

DAYS OF ELIJAH
Irr.

3187   We Fall Down

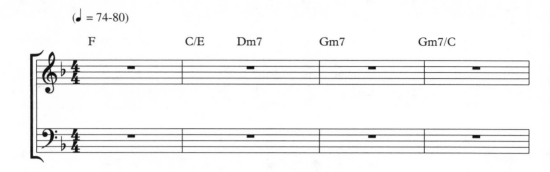

We fall down, we lay our crowns at the feet_

_ of Je - sus; the great - ness of

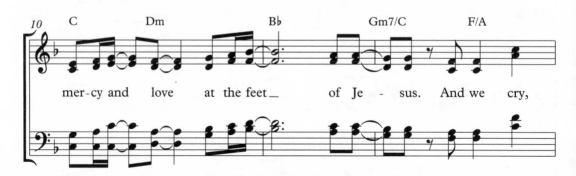

mer-cy and love at the feet_ of Je - sus. And we cry,

WORDS: Chris Tomlin
MUSIC: Chris Tomlin

WE FALL DOWN
Irr.

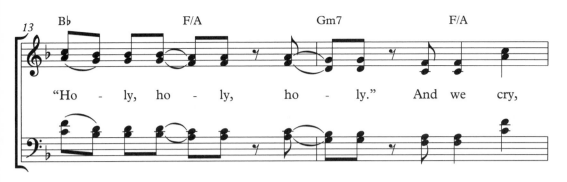

"Ho - ly, ho - ly, ho - ly." And we cry,

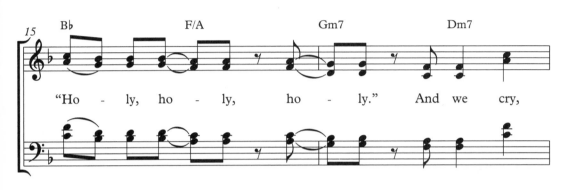

"Ho - ly, ho - ly, ho - ly." And we cry,

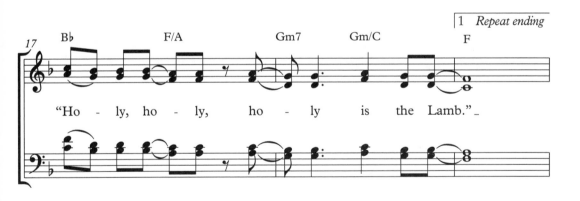

1 Repeat ending

"Ho - ly, ho - ly, ho - ly is the Lamb."

2 Song ending

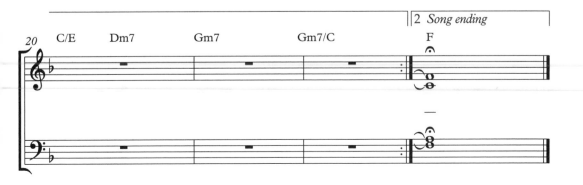

A NEW HEAVEN AND A NEW EARTH

3188

Hosanna

Medium ballad (♩ = 75)

1. I see the King of glo - ry
2. I see a ge - ne - ra - tion

com - ing on the clouds with fire.___ The whole earth shakes,
ris - ing up to take their place___ with self - less faith,___

___ the whole earth shakes.___ I see his love and mer -
___ with self - less faith.___ I see a near re - vi -

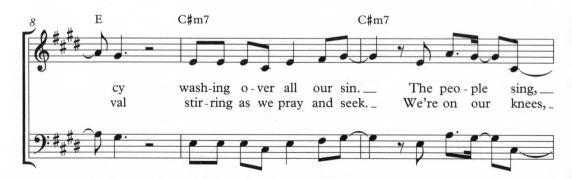

cy   wash - ing o - ver all our sin.___ The peo - ple sing,___
val   stir - ring as we pray and seek.___ We're on our knees,___

WORDS: Brooke Fraser
MUSIC: Brooke Fraser

HILLSONG HOSANNA
Irr.

3189

There Is a Higher Throne

Maestoso ($\quarternote$ = 92)

1. There is a high-er throne than all this world has known, where
2. And there we'll find our home; our life be-fore the throne. We'll

faith-ful ones from ev-ery tongue will one day come.
hon-or him in per-fect song where we be-long.

Be-fore the Son we'll stand, made fault-less through the Lamb; be-
He'll wipe each tear-stained eye as thirst and hun-ger die. The

liev-ing hearts find prom-ised grace; sal-va-tion comes.
Lamb be-comes our Shep-herd King; we'll reign with him.

Refrain

Hear heav-en's voic-es sing; their thun-der-ous an-them rings through

em-er-ald courts and sap-phire skies; their prais-es rise.

WORDS: Keith Getty and Kristyn Lennox Getty
MUSIC: Keith Getty and Kristyn Lennox Getty

HIGHER THRONE
66.84 D with Refrain

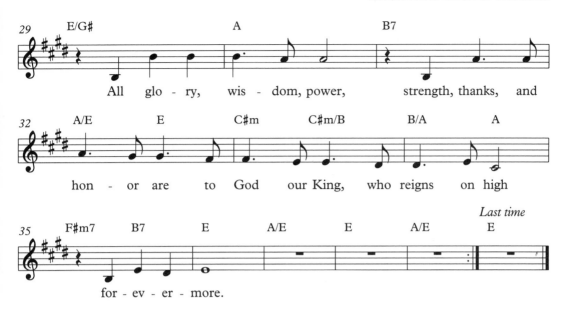

All glo-ry, wis-dom, power, strength, thanks, and
hon-or are to God our King, who reigns on high

Last time

for-ev-er-more.

X-MAS OR LENT ## Mary Had a Little Lamb 3190

1. Ma-ry had a lit-tle Lamb, the
2. Ma-ry saw the Pas-chal Lamb with
3. Ma-ry held the Pas-chal Lamb — I
4. Ma-ry saw the Pas-chal Lamb, her
5. Ma-ry, lo, the lit-tle Lamb, the

ba-by took a nap; the Sav-ior Christ, the great I Am, lay
cross and with a crown; the hill-top held the great I Am, all
am, I was, I will — till Ma-ry knew her own I Am and
own na-ti-vi-ty, re-ceived her in-ner Yes I Am, her
Son is on the throne. The crown is now a di-a-dem and

[1-4]

5

sleep-ing on a lap.
hope came tum-bling down.
Ma-ry's heart grew still.
new pros-per-i-ty.

we are not a-lone.

WORDS: Herbert Brokering
MUSIC: Jackson Henry

THEOTOKOS
76.86

ACKNOWLEDGMENTS

Use of copyrighted material is gratefully acknowledged by the publisher. Every effort has been made to locate the administrator of each copyright. The publisher would be pleased to have any errors or omissions brought to its attention.

Abingdon Press
(see The Copyright Company)

Sally Ahner
1303 Erin Lane
Nashville TN 37221
Phone: (615) 352-3928

Alfred Music Publishing Co., Inc.
Rights & Permissions
P.O. Box 10003
Van Nuys, CA 91410-0003
permissions@alfred.com

Alletrop Music (see Music Services)

Ariose Music/Mountain Spring Music
(see EMICMGPublishing.com)

Ateliers et Presses de Taizé
(see GIA Publications, Inc.)

Augsburg Fortress
Attn: Permissions
P.O. Box 1209
Minneapolis MN 55440-1209
Phone: (800) 328-4646

BMG Songs, Inc./Kid Brothers of St.
Frank Music
(see Music Services)

Bridge Building Music
(see Music Services)

Bud John Songs, Inc.
(see EMI CMG Publishing)

Bud John Tunes, Inc.
(see EMI CMG Publishing)

Carl Fischer, Inc.
65 Bleecker Street
New York, NY 10012
Phone: (212) 777-0900
Fax: (212) 477-6996
All rights assigned to Carl Fischer,
LLC. International copyright secured.
All rights reserved including
performing rights.

Century Oaks Publishing Group/
Richwood Music
(see Conexion Media Group, Inc.)

Susan Palo Cherwien
(see Augsburg Fortress)

Choristers Guild
12404 Park Central Drive
Suite 100
Dallas, TX 75251-1802
(469) 398-3606
(469) 398-3611

Clumsy Fly Music
(see Music Services)

Conexion Media Group, Inc.
1301 16th Ave. South
Nashville TN 37212
Phone: (615) 250-4600
Fax: (615) 250-4699

Curious? Music UK
(see EMICMGPublishing.com)

Daybreak Music, LTD
(see Integrity Music, Inc.)

Rev. Lisa Ann Moss Degrenia
Allendale United Methodist Church
247 Carmen Lane
DeBary, FL 32713
Phone: (727) 688-2837
Fax: (727) 528-8364

Desert Flower Music
P.O. Box 1476
Carmichael CA 95609
Phone: (916) 481-2999
www.strathdee.com

Delores Duffner
(see OCP Publications)

EMICMGPublishing.com
Apply for license at this web site.
All rights reserved. Used by
permission.

EMI CMG Publishing
P.O. Box 5084
Brentwood TN 37204-5084
Phone: (615) 371-4400
All rights reserved. Used by
permission.

Isaac Everett
1 St. Nicholas Terrace #23
New York NY 10027
isaac@isaaceverett.com

Kenneth L. Fenton
3100 85th Avenue, North #227
Brooklyn Park, MN 55443
Phone: (763) 657-7069

Ben Fielding, Reuben Morgan and
Hillsong Publishing
(see Integrity Music, Inc.)

G. Schirmer, Inc.
257 Park Avenue, South
New York NY 10010
Phone: (212) 254-1200
Fax: (212) 254-2013
International copyright secured. All
rights reserved. Used by permission.

Gaither Copyright Management
P.O. Box 737
Alexandria IN 46001
Phone: (765) 724-8233
Fax: (765) 724-8290
Used by permission.

The Rev. F. Richard (Dick) Garland
3 Park Avenue
Derry NH 03038
RevHiker@aol.com

Steve Garnaas-Holmes
271 South Street
Concord NH 03301
stevegarnaasholmes@gmail.com

GIA Publications, Inc.
7404 S. Mason Avenue
Chicago IL 60638
Phone: (800) 442-1358
www.giamusic.com
All rights reserved. Used by
permission.

Carolyn Winfrey Gillette
2606 Salem Drive
Wilmington DE 19808-2198
bcgillette@comcast.net

Gloworks Limited
(see EMICMGPublishing.com)

Rev. William P. (Dick) Gorton
4120 South Mill Avenue
Apartment #E220
Tempe AZ 85282
william@gortonmuse.com

Hal Leonard Corporation
Attn: Copyright Department
7777 West Bluemound Road
P.O. Box 13819
Milwaukee, WI 53213
Fax: (414) 774-3259
hlcopyright@halleonard.com
All rights reserved. International
copyright secured. Used by
permission. Reprinted by permission
of Hal Leonard Corporation.

Dr. Barbara Hamm
P. O. Box 1125
Benicia, CA 94510-4125
mstaize@yahoo.com

Harold Flammer, Inc.
(see Hal Leonard Corporation)

Jackson W. Henry
1267 North Rutherford Blvd.
Murfreesboro, TN 37130
jackson@stmarkstn.org

Bret Hesla
(see Augsburg Fortress)

Hillsong Publishing
(see Integrity Music, Inc.)

Hollis Music, Inc.
c/o The Richmond Organization
266 West 37th Street, 17th Floor
New York NY 1018-6609
Phone: (212) 594-9795
Fax: (212) 594-9782
International copyright secured. Made
in USA. All rights reserved including
public performance for profit. Used by
permission.

Hope Publishing Company
380 South Main Place
Carol Stream IL 60188
Phone: (800) 323-1049
Fax: (630) 665-2552
Apply for license at
www.hopepublishing.com
All rights reserved. Used by
permission

ICEL (International Commission on
English in the Liturgy)
1522 K Street NW
Washington DC 20005-1202
Phone: (202) 347-0800
Fax: (202) 347-1839

Integrity Music, Inc.
1000 Cody Road
Mobile AL 36695
Phone: (251) 633-9000
Fax: (251) 776-5036

Integrity's Hosanna! Music
1000 Cody Road
Mobile AL 36695
Phone: (251) 633-9000
Fax: (251) 776-5036

IzzySolSongs
(see Metro One)

Kid Brothers of St. Frank Publishing
(see Music Services)

Kirkland House Music
(see The Lorenz Corporation)

Marienne Kreitlow
Living Song
7616 25th St. SW
Howard Lake, MN 55349
kreitlow@cmgate.com

Doreen Lankshear-Smith
P.O. Box 10155
Thunder Bay Ontario P7B 6T7
doreenls@web.ca

Latter Rain Music
(see EMICMGPublishing.com)

Les Presses de Taizé
(see GIA Publications, Inc.)

Licensing Associates
935 Broad Street, #31
Bloomfield, NJ 07003
kathleenkarcher@hotmail.com

LifeWay Worship
One LifeWay Plaza
Nashville, TN 37234
All rights reserved. Used by
permission. Apply for license at www.
lifeway.com/PermissionsRequest

Lilly Mack Music
(see EMICMGPublishing.org)

LNWhymns.com
(see The Copyright Company)

Jay D. Locklear
263 Pressly Foushee Road
Sanford, NC 27300
jaylocklear@saintlukeumc.org

Maranatha Praise, Inc.
(see Music Services)

Martin and Morris
(see Alfred Music Publishing Co., Inc.)

Raquel Mora Martinez
14710 Kinsem
San Antonio, TX 78248
JoelRaqM@aol.com

Dean McIntyre
2501 Ravine Dr.
Nashville TN 37217-3614
imdbm@comcast.net

Meaux Mercy
(see Music Services)

Mercy/Vineyard Publishing
(see Music Services)

Metro One
104 Whitefish Hills Drive
Whitefish, MT 59937
brianray@me.com

Mexican-American Cultural Center
(see OCP Publications)

Rev. John Middleton
41 Pine Tree Street
Lexington TN 38351
jbmiddleton@bellsouth.net

Reuben Morgan/Hillsong Publishing
(see Hal Leonard Corporation)

Music Services
5409 Maryland Way
Suite 200
Brentwood, TN 37027
Apply at musicservices.org for license
All rights reserved. Used by
permission.

New Spring Publishing, Inc./Never
Say Never Songs
(see Music Services)

OCP Publications
Attn: Licensing Department
5536 NE Hassalo
Portland OR 97213-3638
Phone: (503) 281-1191
Fax: (503) 282-3486

Oxford University Press
Great Clarendon Street
Oxford UK OX2 6DP
Reproduced by permission of Oxford
University Press. All rights reserved.

Pilot Point Music
(see The Copyright Company)

The Pilgrim Press
700 Prospect Avenue
Cleveland OH 44115-1100
Phone: (216) 736-3757

Phil Posthuma
2840 Dell Ridge Drive
Holt, MI 48842
phil.posthuma@trinitywired.com

Patrick Roache
(see GIA Publications, Inc.)

Sacred Songs
(see Music Services)

Ernest Sands
(see OCP Publications)

Greg Scheer
Church of the Servant
3835 Burton, SE
Grand Rapids, MI 49546
Phone: (616) 956-7611x11

Daniel L. Schutte
(see OCP Publications)

Daniel L. Schutte and New Dawn Music
(see OCP Publications)

Adam Seate
1605 East Pine Street
Goldsboro, NC 27530
adamseate@nccumc.org

Selah Publishing Co., Inc.
4055 Cloverlea Street
Pittsburg, PA 15227
Phone: (412) 886-1020
Fax: (412) 886-1022
All rights reserved. Used by
permission.

Shepherd's Heart Music, Inc.
(see Music Services)

j. snodgrass
509 9th Avenue, West
Hendersonville, NC 28791
Phone: (828) 450-7768

Stainer & Bell Ltd.
(see Hope Publishing Company)

Storm Boy Music
(see Music Services)

Thankyou Music
(see EMICMGPublishing.com)

The Copyright Company
P.O. Box 128139
Nashville TN 37212-8139
Phone: 615-244-9848
Fax: 615-244-9850

The General Board of Discipleship of
The United Methodist Church
1908 Grand Avenue
Nashville TN 37212
Phone: (615) 340-7000

The Iona Community
(see GIA Publications, Inc.)

The Jubilate Group
(see Hope Publishing Company)

The Lorenz Corporation
501 East Third Street
Dayton OH 45401-0802
Phone: (937) 228-6118
Fax: (937) 223-2042

The United Methodist Publishing House
(see The Copyright Company)

Rev. John D. Thornburg
6748 Orangewood
Dallas TX 75248
ethornbu@aol.com

Marilyn E. Thornton
4381 Enchanted Circle
Nashville TN 37218

Josh Tinley
2406 Keeling Drive
Mt. Juliet TN 37122
jtinley@umpublishing.org

Universal Music/MGB Songs
(see Music Services)

Utryck
(see Licensing Associates)

Van Ness Press, Inc.
(see LifeWay Worship)

Vineyard Songs
(see Music Services)

Walton Music Corporation
(see Licensing Associates)

Wayne Leupold Editions, Inc.
8510 Triad Drive
Colfax NC 27235
Phone: (800) 765-3196
wleupold@msn.com

WGRG
(see GIA Publications, Inc.)

William J. Gaither, Inc.
(see Gaither Copyright Management)

Wordspring Music and Songs From
The Indigo Room
(see Music Services)

worshiptogether.com Songs
(see EMICMGPublishing.com)

worshiptogether.com Songs/sixsteps
Music
(see EMICMGPublishing.com)

INDEX OF FIRST LINES AND COMMON TITLES (with Keys)

[K] = major key   [K-K] = beginning-ending keys
[k] = minor key   [K(-K)] = beginning key-optional ending key (or chord)